# FOREW

*Lizzie Borden took an axe*
*And gave her mother forty whacks.*
*When she saw what she had done*
*She gave her father forty-one.*

OR DID SHE? ON AUGUST 4, 1892, SOMEONE brutally murdered Andrew Jackson Borden, age 70, and his wife Abby, age 64, in their Fall River home. One week later, police arrested Andrew Borden's 32-year-old daughter, Lizzie, for the murder of her father and stepmother.

Suspicion centered on Lizzie because she did not show the hysteria expected from a young woman in these circumstances. But during the investigation and the trial, attention also fell on life within the Borden household: although Andrew Borden was a successful man of business, he drove hard bargains and had never spent a foolish dollar. Reporters, detectives, and the curious flocked to Fall River for the sensational trial. A former Massachusetts governor defended Lizzie in the courtroom; outside, some newspapers castigated her character; women's rights activists defended her. The jury deliberated for less than an hour before finding Lizzie Borden not guilty.

Scholar Karen Chaney examines the case of Lizzie Borden, from her life before these tragic events made her family famous, through the investigation and trial, and finally to her long and quiet life afterward. Did Lizzie Borden kill her father and stepmother? If so, why was she acquitted? If not, why did the public mind convict her? Why has she been the subject of childhood rhymes and of plays, opera, and film? In probing these questions we can understand why New England remembers Lizzie Borden.

*Robert J. Allison, Series Editor*
*Boston, Massachusetts*

NEW ENGLAND REMEMBERS

# Lizzie Borden

## Karen Elizabeth Chaney

*Robert J. Allison, Series Editor*

*Commonwealth Editions*
*Beverly, Massachusetts*

ISBN-13: 978-1-889833-81-1
ISBN-10: 1-889833-81-9

**Library of Congress Cataloging-in-Publication Data**
Chaney, Karen Elizabeth.
  Lizzie Borden / Karen Elizabeth Chaney.
    p. cm. — (New England remembers)
  Includes bibliographical references and index.
  ISBN 1-889833-81-9 (alk. paper)
  1. Borden, Lizzie, 1860-1927. 2. Murder—Massachusetts—Fall River—Case studies. I. Title. II. Series.
  HV6534.F2.C47 2006
  364.152'30974485—dc22
                    2006006031

Cover and interior design by Laura McFadden Design, Inc.
laura.mcfadden@rcn.com
Printed in the United States of America.

Commonwealth Editions
266 Cabot Street, Beverly, Massachusetts 01915
www.commonwealtheditions.com

Front cover photo: Lizzie Borden in 1892, the year before the murders of her father and stepmother. The photographer captured both Lizzie's shyness and her flair for elegant fashion. Otherwise unadorned, she wears a simple ring on her right hand. Courtesy of Fall River Historical Society.
Back cover photo: The Borden home on August 4, 1892, the day of the murders. Courtesy of Fall River Historical Society.

The *New England Remembers* series
Robert J. Allison, Series Editor
*The Hurricane of 1938*
*The Big Dig*
*The Cocoanut Grove Fire*
*Sacco and Vanzetti*
*The Boston Strangler*

The "New England Remembers" logo features a photo of the Thomas Pickton House, Beverly, Massachusetts, used courtesy of the Beverly Historical Society.

# CONTENTS

# INTRODUCTION

ON AUGUST 4, 1892, THE RESIDENTS OF FALL RIVER, Massachusetts, went about their daily business in the summer heat. Women went to Frank Sargent's store for the big dry-goods sale and then to Hudnor's Market to buy the fixings for their noon dinner. Men conducted business at the bank while drummers hawked their wares to shop owners. Ice cream peddlers sold their welcome treat to overheated children and adults. After the workday, residents picked up the evening edition of the *Fall River Daily Globe* to find out what had happened in the world.

The front page reported more tragedy in Homestead, Pennsylvania. Strikers at the Carnegie iron mill violently protested the arrest of yard-master James Dovey and superintendent Nevin McCouncil for murder. Congress had finally appropriated the necessary funds for next year's world's fair in Chicago. There was good news on the political front—if you were a Democrat, that is. In Louisville, vice presidential candidate Adlai F. Stevenson reassured supporters that the New York Democrats were united.

In local crime news, Michael Harrington had stolen a watch from William Sheehan while under the influence of spirits, and a judge fined John Duggan fifty dollars for maintaining "a common nuisance."

The real shocker, though, was on page 7. At about eleven o'clock that morning, a young Fall River woman, Lizzie Borden, had walked into the family house on Second Street and found her father's mutilated body on the couch in the sitting room. If that wasn't bad enough, Miss Borden's stepmother, Abby, lay on the floor in the upstairs guest room, her head bashed in with an ax. What made this crime unique was its particular brutality, the victims' identities, and the primary suspect: Miss Lizzie Borden herself.

🪓 🪓 🪓

# CHAPTER ONE

# Cold Mutton, Johnnycakes, and Murder

The Borden residence at 92 Second Street was by no means pretentious. Built in 1845, it was originally a double tenement house, located in the "flats" of Fall River. The "flats" were an unpleasant neighborhood in the southern part of the city, next to iron mills and factories. By the time Andrew Borden purchased the house in 1871, he had amassed a considerable fortune through shrewd investments in real estate and the cotton textile industry, and through his own strict frugality and unscrupulous business tactics. Why would such an up-and-comer in the Fall River business community choose to live in the flats rather than the more fashionable "Hill"? Perhaps it was because the Second Street house reflected Andrew's character, his distaste for society, and his desire to live closer to his business interests. The neighborhood, within blocks of City Hall, was a hodgepodge of businesses, private homes, pool halls, and immigrant tenements. It also was plagued by a fair amount of crime. In June 1891, burglars had brazenly broken into the Bordens' home in broad daylight, when some of the family were at home. Somehow the burglars were familiar with the house's layout and targeted Mr. Borden's second-floor desk. They stole some money, horse-car tickets, and Mrs. Borden's gold watch. Although Andrew Borden reported the robbery, the police never arrested anyone.

On Tuesday evening, August 2, 1892, Andrew, his second wife, Abby, and Andrew's thirty-two-year-old daughter, Lizzie, sat down for their usual sparse supper of milk and baker's bread. Emma, the elder daughter, was away in Fairhaven, visiting her friend Helen Brownell and her mother. While many of her friends described Lizzie as a shy, well-bred young woman, others considered her aloof and cold. At about nine o'clock, the family fell desperately ill, vomiting continually throughout the night. Both Andrew and Abby were convinced that someone had poisoned them. When the Bordens awoke the next morning, they still felt sick. Abby decided, in spite of her husband's protests, to call on their family doctor, Seabury Bowen. The close-fisted Andrew Borden had no intention of lining the old quack's pockets with his money. As Abby left the house at eight o'clock in the morning, headed for Dr. Bowen's house across the street, her husband angrily shouted, "Well, my money shan't pay for it!"

Around eleven-thirty that same Wednesday morning, a young woman walked into D. R. Smith's Drug Store at the corner of South Main and Columbia. Pharmacist Eli Bence thought she looked familiar and later said that he was struck "by a peculiar expression around the eyes." When she asked one of the clerks for ten cents' worth of prussic acid to treat a seal cape, Bence stepped in. While prussic acid was used to kill fleas and ants, it had no practical application to leather or fur. It was also a lethal poison. Massachusetts law required that all purchasers have a doctor's prescription and that pharmacists keep a log of all sales to prevent illegal use. The young woman, it turned out, had no prescription, so Bence refused the sale. She argued that she had purchased it several times in the past, to treat a seal cape. Bence, however, was adamant. He reported later that he said, "Well, my dear lady, it is something we don't sell unless by a prescription from the doctor, as it is a dangerous thing to handle." After the young woman left, someone told Bence that she was Andrew Borden's daughter Lizzie. Other druggists in the area reported that a woman fitting Lizzie's description had also tried to buy prussic acid from them the previous Monday.

According to her own account, however, Lizzie kept to her room much of that Wednesday. At about one o'clock in the afternoon, she heard conversation downstairs and recognized the voice of her uncle, John V. Morse, whom she hadn't seen for months. Morse, whose sister

*Lizzie as a young woman. She loved the theater, but rejected it for a higher calling to the church, primarily because she wanted to feel useful and accepted. After her trial, church women cruelly snubbed her. She then turned her back on the church and rekindled her love for the theater. (Fall River Historical Society)*

was Lizzie's mother, had been living in Iowa, a successful farmer and horse trader. He had returned east to help an old friend run a meat business in nearby Dartmouth. When Morse appeared unexpectedly at the Bordens' side door, Andrew and Abby invited him to midday dinner. Afterward, he sat talking with them until four in the afternoon. Lizzie overheard the conversation while she rested in her room. Because the noise of their voices disturbed her, she closed her door.

Needing some fresh air around seven o'clock in the evening, Lizzie decided to visit her close friend Alice Russell, who lived nearby at 33 Borden Street. Lizzie told Alice that she had a premonition that something horrible was about to happen. She was convinced that someone had poisoned the family on Tuesday night, which is why the three of them had become so ill. It could have been any one of her father's many enemies, she said. Lord knows he had his fair share! Recently, Lizzie had heard her father arguing with a prospective tenant who wanted to rent one of his commercial properties for a liquor store, which her father found objectionable. Lizzie left her friend's house a few minutes before nine and went directly to bed when she arrived home.

John Morse had returned earlier, while Lizzie was visiting her friend, and sat up talking with the Bordens until ten o'clock, when he, Abby, and Andrew retired. Morse went up to the guest chamber on the second floor, directly next to Lizzie's room, while Andrew and Abby went up the back stairs to their room. Bridget "Maggie" Sullivan, the twenty-five-year-old kitchen maid, returned from visiting friends a few minutes past ten and noticed that everyone had gone to bed. She took a glass of milk and her oil lamp and walked up the back stairs to her third-floor room. So ended the last peaceful day at 92 Second Street.

At six-fifteen on Thursday morning, Maggie awoke with a nagging headache and did not relish another day of household chores, especially in the summer heat. As the morning sun beat down on the house, Maggie dressed and walked down the back stairs into the kitchen and then into the cellar to collect wood for the kitchen stove. Unlocking the side door, she took in the milk that had sat on the stoop since four o'clock. Soon after that, the iceman came to fill the chest next to the pantry.

By seven-fifteen, Abby and Andrew Borden and John Morse had arisen and were eating a simple breakfast of johnnycakes, mutton, and soup in the dining room. The two men continued talking after breakfast, while Maggie and Abby began their daily chores. When Morse left at approximately eight-fifty, Andrew Borden walked him to the side entrance and suggested that Morse stop at Daniel Emery's house at No. 4 Weybosset to visit Morse's teenage niece and nephew. He unlocked the door and said, "John, come back to dinner with us." Lizzie did not surface that morning until around nine o'clock. She walked downstairs dressed in a navy blue Bengalese silk skirt and blouse. She noticed her father reading the *Providence Journal* in the sitting room and her stepmother dusting in the dining room. When Maggie asked if she wanted breakfast, Lizzie answered that she didn't feel well enough to eat. Abby told Lizzie that she had gotten a note from a sick friend that morning and was going out to visit her. At around nine-thirty, Abby went upstairs to make up Morse's room. Shortly thereafter, Andrew Borden left the house.

Lizzie decided to eat a couple of cookies and to prepare flats for ironing. After that, Maggie started washing the outside windows.

An hour later, at ten-thirty, Maggie was working in the sitting room when she heard Andrew Borden ring the bell. Realizing that he couldn't get in, she fumbled with the locks to open the door. She thought she heard a laugh from the second-floor landing that sounded like Lizzie. When Borden came into the kitchen, Lizzie was sitting there reading and asked him about the mail. "Nothing for you," he said. Lizzie told her father that Mrs. Borden had received a note from a sick friend and had gone out to visit her. Andrew then walked into the sitting room

*Andrew Borden, Lizzie's father, earned a questionable reputation as a tight-fisted, abstemious businessman, who, in his early career as an under-taker, cut off the legs of tall corpses to fit them into caskets. (Fall River Historical Society)*

*Andrew Borden's second wife, Abby Durfee Gray, was a frugal house-keeper and the stepmother for his two young daughters. (Fall River Historical Society)*

and changed his coat to a cardigan. He lay down on the couch to rest, twisting his body a little so his feet touched the floor. Lizzie asked if he wanted the shades lowered or if she could get him anything, but he declined. Lizzie returned to her ironing, but the flats had cooled down.

About fifteen minutes later, Lizzie walked out back to the barn to look for fishing sinkers. An avid angler, she planned to join a fishing party in Marion on Monday. Before entering the barn, she stopped long enough to pick three pears from the tree nearest the barn. As she opened the door, the stifling heat overwhelmed her, but in spite of her still-queasy stomach, Lizzie climbed up to the loft. Failing to find the sinkers, she walked to the window to eat the pears. She thought she heard a noise from the house. She returned to the house, took off her hat, laid it on the dining room table, and headed upstairs to rest. As she passed the sitting room, she noticed that someone had closed the door, which was usually open. As she pushed it open, she saw her father's body on the sofa, motionless. Then she saw blood. Recoiling, she paused and walked to the back stairs to call for Maggie: "Go for Dr. Bowen as soon as you can. I think Father is hurt."

When Dr. Bowen returned from his rounds, his wife immediately sent him over to the Bordens. He saw Lizzie in the kitchen, and she told him that her father was in the sitting room. Bowen pushed open the door and saw Borden laying on the couch. Andrew Borden was far worse than just hurt. His face had been so badly beaten with a sharp object that he was unrecognizable. There were numerous deep cuts on his head and face; one cut had penetrated his brain. Brain matter protruded from his skull, and one eyeball was severed. Within minutes, people gathered at the Borden residence. Dr. Bowen was there, of course; so was the Bordens' neighbor, Mrs. Adelaide Churchill, and a reporter, John Manning from the *Fall River Daily Globe*. After word reached the police station, marshal Rufus Hilliard sent an officer, George Allen, to the crime scene.

After Dr. Bowen had examined the crime scene in the sitting room, Lizzie asked him to telegraph her sister, Emma, in Fairhaven, but to word

*Police photo of Andrew Borden's murder scene. Borden's body seems oddly posed, with his bloody head resting comfortably against the pillow, his hands on his chest, and his feet touching the floor. (Fall River Historical Society)*

the message discreetly so as not to unduly alarm Helen Brownell's elderly mother. Bowen drove to the telegraph office and then returned to the Borden home.

Lizzie's friend Alice Russell arrived to take charge. As more onlookers, friends, and investigators converged, Lizzie sat in the rocking chair in the kitchen and laid her head on Alice's shoulder. She was apparently in such shock that she didn't recognize Dr. Bowen's wife when the lady came to help.

Lizzie suddenly remembered her stepmother. She raised her head and said, "I wish someone would go and try to find Mrs. Borden."

Mrs. Churchill followed a reluctant Maggie up the front stairs. Halfway up the stairs, they could see across the guest room floor. Mrs. Churchill thought she saw a prostrate figure on the floor, but she wasn't sure because it was too dark to see anything clearly.

*The scene of Abby Borden's murder. At about nine-thirty in the morning, Mrs. Borden was upstairs cleaning the guest bedroom when the murderer attacked, continually striking her with an ax long after the fatal blow was inflicted. No one heard her large two-hundred-pound body hit the floor. (Fall River Historical Society)*

*Crime scene photo of Abby's body from the side with the blood seeping into the rug. The dressing table mirror reflects the police camera. Dr. Seabury Bowen thought Abby Borden may have fainted from fright, but when police officers rolled the body over they discovered that she had been murdered. Officer Doherty screamed, "My God, her face is all smashed in."* *(Fall River Historical Society)*

"That must be her," she said to Maggie, realizing that perhaps Abby had been murdered also. Mrs. Churchill told the police that "I then rushed downstairs, and entering the dining room, I doubled myself up, and uttered an exclamation of fright." After they returned to the dining room, Alice asked, "Is there another?"

Dr. Bowen then went upstairs and saw someone lying on the floor wedged between the dresser and the bed. Although it was dark, he quickly realized that it was Abby Borden. Perhaps she had just fainted, he thought, so he walked around the bed and looked more closely. He saw no blood or any evidence of violence, but he realized that she had not just fainted—that she was probably dead. When he returned to the kitchen, Bowen told Lizzie that someone had killed her stepmother. Lizzie swooned. Bowen and Mrs. Churchill helped her upstairs to her room.

In the meantime, Officer Patrick Doherty and reporter John Manning were the first to examine the scene of Andrew Borden's murder.

Bowen led them both to the sitting room and pulled back the sheet, revealing the body. A reporter later wrote in the *Fall River Daily Globe* that an unidentified veteran police officer told him that he suspected the perpetrator was a woman, because "no one but a crazed woman would commit such a deed as by which Mr. Borden went into eternity." A man would have struck more systematically and forcefully and "would have cut deeper every time he struck and would crush rather than cut his victim."

Doherty and Manning then went upstairs to check on Abby Borden. They pulled the bed toward the door to give themselves more room and then rolled the body over. They were shocked to see her face smashed in as if someone had beaten her with a heavy object. The murderer had brutally struck Mrs. Borden's head, perhaps with an ax, leaving eighteen distinct wounds, some deeper than others, smashing bone and ripping hair. As the killer struck the blows, blood spattered the walls and began to seep into the carpet. Medical experts later determined that the assault—which had probably taken place between nine-thirty and ten o'clock—had continued long after Mrs. Borden was dead.

Rumors and theories quickly circulated. One suggested that Mrs. Borden had witnessed her husband's murder and then had run upstairs to the guest room, where the murderer found and killed her. Others thought anarchists were involved. Maggie immediately implicated one of Borden's Portuguese farmhands, and Lizzie mentioned the prospective tenant who had lashed out at her father for refusing to rent him a store. While the police considered Lizzie, Morse, and Maggie as possible suspects, they ruled out Emma because she was in Fairhaven. The police immediately followed other leads, including Portuguese horse traders and a man who promised to "fix" Borden for cheating him.

As crowds gathered and the police continued their investigation, Lizzie remained secluded in her room. Her sister, Emma, back from Fairhaven, contacted the family attorney, Andrew Jennings. As evening fell on the poorly lit street, the drab gray house looked even more sinister than usual. The mutilated bodies of Andrew and Abby Borden lay in the dining room, where just a few hours earlier they had eaten their last meal of soup, cold mutton, and johnnycakes.

# CHAPTER TWO

# Private Becomes Public

O n Friday morning, August 5, crowds gathered around 92 Second Street in hopes of catching a glimpse of the comings and goings inside. Emma and her uncle John Morse came downstairs and walked past the dining room, which was now the "room of death," to the kitchen. While they ate breakfast, Lizzie remained in her room.

The police gathered early to search the Borden property for clues. They went into the barn looking for footprints on the dusty floor that might confirm Lizzie's alibi, but they found none. Lizzie told the police that she was in the barn looking for fishing sinkers when her father was killed. By nine-thirty, they had discovered nothing else significant.

Meanwhile, reporters fanned out across the city, eagerly following up every rumor and lead, often ahead of the police. While Alice Russell ran the house, John Morse (himself a suspect) acted as the family's spokesperson. Several rumors circulated that Morse had conspired with Lizzie to murder the Bordens. Whenever he left the house, plainclothes police officers, reporters on the qui vive, and a curious public shadowed him.

At one point during the day, Morse asked Dr. William Dolan, the medical examiner, for permission to bury the bloody clothes and sheets in the backyard. According to the *Boston Globe*, he was upset that the "bloody clothing of the victims and the sheeting used to cover them" was still in the house as an unpleasant reminder to Lizzie and Emma. Dolan had at first objected because they were evidence, but eventually he acquiesced. He dug the items up a week later and placed them in a trunk. At five-thirty in the evening, the crowd's morbid curiosity was rewarded when the undertaker and his assistant carried the blood-stained sofa through the front door to store as evidence.

At eight o'clock, Morse left the house and started down Second Street toward Pleasant. As soon as spectators recognized him, they began to follow him. As he crossed Pleasant Street, interested people from City Hall and other neighboring streets joined the pursuit. By the time he reached Bedford Street, the crowd had swelled to about five hundred. Morse stopped to chat with a woman dressed in black, but when the mob descended on them, she quickly vanished. Morse seemed oblivious to the noise, and he continued to the post office to mail a letter. By the time he returned home, the crowd that followed him had swelled to an estimated two thousand people. The police posted more officers

*The Borden home on August 4, 1892, the day of the murders. Lizzie said she had been in the barn, looking for fishing sinkers and eating pears, when the murders occurred. (Fall River Historical Society)*

at the house to protect the family from potential violence. The activity had so unnerved Maggie that she decided to spend the night at Dr. Bowen's house across the street.

The next morning, with more than two thousand people gathered outside the house, three ministers and the undertaker arrived for the funeral. The two caskets were covered with black cloth in the sitting room; Andrew Borden's had a simple ivy wreath on top, and Abby's had a bouquet of white roses, ferns, and pea blossoms. After Reverend Walker Jubb of the Central Congregational Church conducted a simple service of prayer and scripture, the funeral party prepared to go to the Oak Grove Cemetery. As the front door opened, the crowd saw the leaders of Fall River's business community emerge as Borden's pallbearers. The pallbearers had arrived earlier to attend the funeral. Reporters, artists, photographers, and the public pushed to get a better view.

After loading the caskets onto the horse-drawn hearse, the men went back inside, closing the door behind them. Where were Lizzie and Emma? The crowd held its collective breath as the door once again opened. There was Lizzie, with the undertaker supporting her arm as she walked down the front steps, and there was Emma, close behind, visibly shaken and staring straight through the crowd. The sisters were not wearing traditional mourning clothes, which made some of the onlookers complain that they were not showing proper respect. The funeral party rode to the cemetery and left after a brief service. The workmen loaded the coffins back onto the hearse for the short drive to the cemetery vault for post-mortem examinations.

Later in the afternoon, the police returned to the Borden house for a thorough search from the attic down. In the guest room where Mrs. Borden was killed, the searchers saw a blood stain in the corner "where the ill-fated victim fell, and where the life-blood colored the floor a deep crimson," according to a reporter for the Boston Globe. Finding a hard lump in the mattress, police slit it open with a knife, but they found it was nothing more than the product of "long use and insufficient shaking."

The police next moved to Lizzie's room, which was directly next to the guest room. Lizzie had comfortably furnished her room with rich dark wallpaper, "handsome red portieres" (curtains) at the doors, tasteful drapes, and a spotless white bedspread and pillows that reflected the "precise and trim characteristics of its occupant." The room was filled with comfortable easy chairs, rockers, engravings, a well-stocked bookcase, and a few photographs. The police indelicately scrutinized every object in the room, including Lizzie's undergarments. They discovered nothing more than what they assumed was a bloodstain on one of the skirts.

Emma's room was more Spartan, with a single bed, a desk, and some easy chairs. Here again they found nothing unusual. They proceeded to Mr. and Mrs. Borden's room in the back of the house. In contrast to Lizzie's stylish furnishings, theirs was sparsely appointed with outdated furniture. The investigators inspected the first-floor rooms and the cellar, but after three hours they had found nothing more incriminating than the skirt with an unidentified bloodstain.

While Emma and Lizzie offered a $5,000 reward for any information leading to an arrest, the police pursued numerous leads. Dr. Benjamin Handy reported that he had seen an odd man lurking around the Borden house at ten-thirty on the day of the murder. The man's "weird and horrible" expression caused Handy to think the man was "just nerving himself to go in and commit a crime." Lizzie quickly exonerated the Portuguese farmhand who she said was actually a Swede, defending him as a loyal employee who had served the Borden family well. The police also ruled out the disgruntled tenant who wanted to rent Borden's store as a rum shop.

Another group of possible suspects had been evicted from the top floor of Borden's Ferry Street property. Mrs. Ryan, an Irish immigrant, had lived there with her large family. Already crowded with Ryans, the apartment overflowed with illegal borders to whom Mrs. Ryan rented rooms. Mr. Simmons, the first-floor tenant, complained that the Ryans raided his strawberry patch, kept roving dogs, and allowed water to leak into his apartment. The Ryans' reported drunkenness had especially upset Borden, who was a staunch teetotaler. When Borden personally evicted the family, Mrs. Ryan "set upon him so vigorously with her tongue that he beat a retreat." Another tenant, Mr. LaCombe, overheard Mrs. Ryan shout, "I wish he was dead. I would like to hear of his death." It seems that Mrs. Ryan had openly voiced what some people secretly wished.

One by one, the police ruled out these leads and narrowed their focus to "near home" theories. On the day after the murders, the story broke about Lizzie's alleged visit to Smith's Drug Store to purchase the sofa where he laid. The door next to that leads to the yard, and the right-hand door leads to the kitchen.

the store within 36 hours past
uired for a certain poison.
k was asked to accompany the
l closely questioned as to the
relative to the time, the girl's
entally, the amount and quality
n she had bought, or called for,
ers then led the drug clerk to
1 2d st. where Miss Lizzie was
r the time being. The young
not previously well acquainted
ung woman, but he told them
ld identify her at sight.
lentify her, and in the presence
e officers info
is place of bus ness and made
a bottle of poison.
den's reply to t is accusation, as
exact language which was used
is known only the two police-
rself.
ement above ma de is absolutely
was verified in every particular
reporter last ight within 10
er it happened.

CE AT THE DOORS.

Everybody Who Comes and
Goes at House.
ER, Mass., Aug. .—In the closely
dining-room f the Borden
on 2d t. are the
e victims of yes erday's tragedy,
tomorrow with brief burial ser-
signed to the g ave.
nt door is a poli e officer whose
are to pass o one into the
ss in authority, ithout the con-
family.
1 officer sta s in a shel-
k at the fear of the
for what urpose cannot
he rear fence s fully 25 feet
could scarcel be scaled with
ladder.
rd sentinel is the outer gate,
o keep the sid walk clear and
vel.
d of men, women and
are braving a severe
s forenoon for he privilege of
n the street a d watching the
tragedy.
them are offi ers in citizens'
o are instructe to shadow and
ely any memb r of the house-
ay go out.
e of importance has transpired
e house this morning. The
re astir at 6. 0 o'clock, and
hour l
d. There were the Misses
r. Morse and a lady friend
aughters present, and from
nts of the serv ant girl, Bridget
ey ate but little and talked less.
na Borden, who was absent from
e time of the tragedy, returned
day afternoon. She appears
nd self-possessed, and was seen
ing and interviewed by
1 the case. Miss Lizzie
yet decided to speak
tion, and has denied all press
interview. The city marshal
her today and take her state-

The police are not working on outside rumors, for there are none.
Miss Lizzie Borden met with an accident of a serious nature last winter. A dumb waiter fell, striking her across the hands. It was very remarkable that she escaped without broken wrists. It was accounted for on the ground that she had unusually strong and large limbs. Her hands and arms are as muscular as a man's. She weighs about 180 pounds and is physically strong.
Physicians think it is physically wonderful, and to her credit that she passed through the ordeal of finding her father's body without fainting, as most women would have done.

that there is a story still to be told in the case.
The sale of GLOBES this morning was unprecedented. The news stands and boys upon the street found a demand even greater than the supply on hand.

## $5000 REWARD

Offered by the Daughters of the Murdered Man and Wife.

FALL RIVER, Mass., Aug. 5.—Just before noon the following advertisement was received at the office of the Fall River Globe:

$5000 REWARD.

The above reward will be paid to any one who will secure the arrest and conviction of the person or persons who occasioned the death of Mr. Andrew J. Borden and his wife.

(Signed)           EMMA J. BORDEN.
                   LIZZIE A. BORDEN.

To ascertain how the above announcement came about, a GLOBE representative called upon the Borden family.
Mr. Morse said: "Emma and Lizzie felt they ought to do something as an incentive for the police. They are anxious that the guilty parties be captured at the earliest possible moment They will spare neither money nor time to hunt down the murderers. Their lives will, if necessary, be devoted to the work. That is all I care to say."
Neither of the ladies feel equal to being interviewed.
Mr. Morse added that the funeral arrangements had just been completed. Services will be held at the house tomorrow at 11 o'clock, Rev. E. A. Buck, the city missionary, will officiate. The interment will be at Oak Grove cemetery.

## "MONEY THE MOTIVE."

Brother-in-Law of Borden Tells of Interview with Daughter.

FALL RIVER, Mass., Aug. 5.—Hiram Harrington, a blacksmith and brother-in-law of Andrew J. Borden, the murdered man, has an extensive knowledge of the family affairs. Mr. Harrington is married to Lurana, the only sister of Mr. Borden. When interviewed this morning at his shop he said:
"My wife being an only sister, was very fond of Mr. Borden and always subservient to his will, and by her intimacy with his affairs I have become acquainted with a good deal of the family history during years past.
"Mr. Borden was an exceedingly hard man, concerning money matters, determined and stubborn, and when once he got an idea nothing could change him. He was too hard for me.

"Have you been asked for such a conference?" he was asked.
"No; so far as I know, there is no foundation for the report that I was to meet Mr. Reid. I think the advance agents for this show got muddled."
"There has been much talk about the President-placating you. Has any proposition of that kind been made?" Mr. Platt was asked.
"No, I know nothing about this placating business, only what I read in the newspapers. I don't want to be placated. I have not asked anything of President Harrison since the campaign opened, and I am not going to ask anything of him."
"Have you been asked to meet the President when he comes to the city?"
"I have not."
"Will you say anything about the political situation in the State?"
"Yes, the situation is all right, so far as I know."
"Is the Republican machine working smoothly and in the interest of Harrison?"
"I guess so. Don't know, though, I haven't been up the State for two weeks."
"Who is running the machine?"
"Oh, Hackett, I guess, he's chairman of the campaign committee, you know."
"It is said Senator, that ex-Secretary Blaine has been won over and will make a speech for the President. Do you know anything about that?"
"Well, I have observed that all Mr. Blaine's speeches so far have been made through the newspapers. I guess I'll be making speeches for Harrison as soon as Mr. Blaine will."
"Is the President coming to New York to look into the political situation here?"
"I don't know. I have no information to that effect."
"Is the Republican party harmonious in the State of New York?"
"So far as I know it is."
Mr. Platt concluded the interview by stating in a very positive manner that he would not confer with Mr. Reid on the political situation and that he had not been invited to attend any Republican love feast.

## JOHN ORVIS' ADVICE.

Labor Voters Should Unite on One Party.

John Orvis of Roxbury, who was nominated for governor by the Socialistic Labor party, on Aug. 1 has declined the nomination. He says: "The gravity of the situation makes it unwise, if not perilous, to divide the labor vote. It seems to me that there should be a concentration of all the labor forces upon a single party."

## DEMOCRATS ORGANIZE.

A Campaign Club for Cleveland and Stevenson Formed.

EXETER, N. H., Aug. 5.—A well-attended meeting of the Democrats of Exeter occurred last evening at the Squamscott House to organize a Cleveland and Stevenson Club for the campaign.
The meeting was called to order by A. B. Fowler, and H. S. Scammon acted as temporary secretary.
A permanent organization was effected, consisting as follows: President, A. B. Fowler; vice-presidents, Charles H. Towle, Andrew J. Brown, George F. Haynes, Joseph J. Hallinan, Edward E. Nowell, J. P. Dwyer, James E. Cahill, S. Roswell Peavy; secretary, John O'Neill; treasurer, H. H. Taylor.
A committee to present bylaws and constitution, consisting of John O'Neill, Louis E. Mayers and E. E. Nowell was appointed to report at a meeting to be called by the

*Offer of a $5,000 reward, published in the* **Boston Globe** *on August 5, 1892. John Morse, the family representative, assured the* **Globe** *that Lizzie and Emma Borden would spare "neither money nor time to hunt down the murderers." (Boston Public Library)*

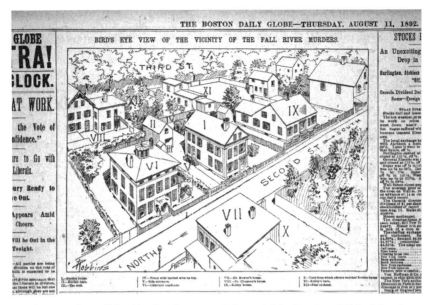

*Bird's-eye view of the Borden house and the neighborhood, published by the* Boston Globe *as a visual guide for its readers during the early investigation. (Boston Public Library)*

poison. Lizzie vehemently denied the visit, claiming that she had been in her room all day nursing a sick stomach.

The formal inquest began five days after the murder, on August 9. A uniformed policeman arrived at the Borden home to escort Lizzie to the courthouse. The *Boston Globe* reported that she had aged considerably since the tragedy, except for her "bright eyes and haughty expression." Over the next three days, District Attorney Hosea Knowlton examined evidence and questioned witnesses behind closed doors to determine if a crime had been committed and to identify possible suspects. Although the police had suspected Morse, Mrs. Daniel Emery told police Morse had been at her house from nine-thirty to eleven-thirty to visit family on the morning of the crime.

Lizzie's appearance at the inquest was the only time she testified during the entire ordeal. Lizzie waived her legal right to testify at trial. She remained calm and poised during the questioning. At times, she answered that she did not remember or did not know how to answer Knowton's questions. He pressed her about her relationship with her stepmother, her dress, her whereabouts when her father returned from downtown and also about her alleged visit to the barn.

When Knowlton asked about her relationship with her stepmother, Lizzie became guarded and defensive.

"Did you ever have any trouble with your stepmother?"

"No, sir," she answered.

Lizzie then told him that she had had a "difference of opinion" with Abby five years earlier over property, but nothing more serious.

"You have been on pleasant terms with your stepmother since then?"

"Yes, sir," she answered.

She went on to say that they weren't the "dearest of friends," but cordial.

When asked if the relationship was like a mother and daughter, Lizzie answered "in some ways it was, and in some way it was not."

Knowlton then asked her "in what ways was it not."

"I did not call her Mother."

After the property dispute, she chose not "to call her Mother."

When pressed why, Lizzie answered, "I haven't any reason to give, except that I did not want to." She refused to expand her answer, because she did not "know what to say."

Knowlton then asked what she was wearing on the day of the murder.

"I had on a navy blue sort of a bengaline; or India silk skirt, with a navy blue blouse. In the afternoon they thought I had better change it. I put on a pink wrapper."

Knowlton pointed out that when Andrew Borden returned home, Maggie said she had heard Lizzie laughing from the second-floor landing, whereas Lizzie claimed she was in the kitchen reading an old magazine.

"Where were you when he returned?" Knowlton asked.

"I was down in the kitchen reading an old magazine that had been left in the cupboard, an old *Harper's* magazine."

"You remember, Miss Borden, I will call your attention to it so as to see if I have any misunderstanding, not for the purpose of confusing you; you remember that you told me several times that you were downstairs, and not upstairs when your father came home? You have forgotten, perhaps?"

*A wide-eyed Lizzie in profile, circa 1890. During the trial, a society lady told Lizzie's friend Mary Livermore that she knew Lizzie was guilty because her picture in the newspapers "was that of a murderess."*
*(Fall River Historical Society)*

A confused Lizzie answered, "I don't know what I have said. I have answered so many questions that I am so confused I don't know one thing from another. I am telling you just as nearly as I know."

"Which now is your recollection of the true statement of the matter, that you were downstairs when the bell rang and your father came?"

"I think I was downstairs in the kitchen."

"And then you were not upstairs."

"I think I was not, because I went upstairs immediately, as soon as I went down, and then came down again and stayed down.

He ended the day with questions about the note Mrs. Borden allegedly received.

"Did you ever see the note?" Knowlton asked.

"No, sir."

"She said she was going out that morning?"

"Yes, sir."

The court session ended at six in the evening. The next day, August 10, Lizzie returned. Knowlton asked her about her visit to the barn, which took place at about the time of her father's murder. Lizzie said she had eaten three pears in the barn. Knowlton asked her how she had been feeling that morning.

"Better than I did the night before," Lizzie answered.

"You were feeling better than you were in the morning?"

"I felt better in the morning than I did the night before."

"That is not what I asked you," he said. "You were then, when you were in that hot loft, looking out of the window and eating three pears, feeling better, were you not, than you were in the morning when you could not eat any breakfast?"

"I never eat any breakfast," Lizzie answered.

"You did not answer my question, and you will, if I have to put it all day. Were you, then when you were eating those pears in that hot loft, looking out of that closed window, feeling better than you were in the morning when you ate no breakfast?"

"I was feeling well enough to eat the pears."

Knowlton kept at her until she didn't know what to say.

"I don't know how to answer you, because I told you I felt better in the morning anyway."

Knowlton also rattled Lizzie with gruesome questions about the discovery of her father's body.

"You saw his face covered with blood?"

"Yes, sir."

"Did you see the eyeball hanging out?"

"No, sir."

"See the gashes where his face was laid open?"

"No, sir."

The court stenographer indicated that Lizzie covered her face with her hand for a minute before resuming testimony.

Knowlton then asked Lizzie about her knowledge of hatchets. Lizzie answered that she knew of hatchets in the cellar but that she never used them. When asked about the possibility of blood on any hatchets, Lizzie said she didn't know. Her father had killed pigeons in May or June, but he usually twisted their necks off.

Knowlton then returned to the dress. Lizzie told him that she had given the officers the same navy blue silk dress that she wore on the morning of the murders. When asked about possible bloodstains on the garments, she attributed them to flea bites.

Knowlton adjourned the hearing at twelve-thirty and excused Lizzie and Morse. Lizzie was obviously shaken from the questioning. When she emerged "from the Matron's room she was tear-stained and very much upset," acccording to the *Boston Globe*. Both Hosea Knowlton and Rufus Hilliard considered Lizzie the chief suspect and her testimony did nothing to change their opinion. After all, he had heard that Lizzie had a contentious relationship with her stepmother, her alibi was uncorroborated, and she was alone in the house with the victims. Although he felt the case against her was strong, Knowlton had his sights on the state attorney general's office, so he wanted to make sure to proceed cautiously. To avoid further criticism about police persecution, he decided to question Lizzie further before making an arrest.

Therefore at three-fifteen on August 11, just one week after the murders, Marshal Hilliard arrived with a carriage to bring Lizzie to the courthouse. He was shocked at how much Lizzie's appearance had changed. She looked lifeless, as if she were fading away. She walked out of the house with Emma and her friend, Mrs. Mary Brigham, and "bowed mechanically" to Hilliard. Once in the carriage, she closed her eyes and slumped back onto the pillow. Emma, in contrast, was highly agitated, but as a member of "a reserved and self-contained family," she regained her composure.

At the courthouse, Lizzie once again took the stand.

Knowlton asked her if the visit to Smith's Drug Store had occurred, as Eli Bence had testified earlier at the inquest.

"It did not," Lizzie answered.

"Did you go into any drug store and inquire for prussic acid?" "I did not."

Knowlton returned to the events of Thursday, August 4. Unable to shake Lizzie from her previous testimony, he changed strategy. He reminded her that the purpose of his questioning was not to confuse her but to "find the author of this tragedy."

"I now ask you if you can furnish any other fact, or give any other, even suspicion, that will assist the officers in any way in this matter," he said.

Lizzie remembered that about two weeks earlier as she was returning from Alice Russell's house around nine o'clock, she "saw a shadow on the side steps." As she slowed down, "somebody ran down the steps, around the east end of the house. I thought it was a man, because I saw no skirts, and I was frightened, and of course I did not go around to see." Lizzie ran into the house through the front entrance and locked the door. Although she never told her father, she had mentioned the incident to Andrew Jennings, the family lawyer, and the Pinkerton detective O. M. Hanscom after the murders. She now had remembered that a similar incident had taken place the previous winter. She had returned from church on a Thursday night and had seen a short, unidentifiable man run around the house and disappear into the dark.

Lizzie's testimony did nothing to change Hilliard's and Knowlton's opinion that she had murdered her parents. She was taken to a drab seven-by-ten-foot cell on the second floor of the Fall River Police Station. As soon as Andrew Jennings heard about the imminent arrest, he raced to the police station. When he entered the room, he saw Lizzie, lying seemingly comatose on the couch, with Emma nearby. Jennings looked at Emma and then at Lizzie, according to a newspaper account, "with her eyes closed and face thinner and paler than ever." Jennings spoke as gently and softly to Lizzie as possible, telling her of her impending arrest. The newspaper reported that her pale skin against the black dress seemed to emphasize her death-like state, "as if her spirit had passed beyond the grave and the frail spark of vitality was extinguished." Emma burst into tears, kissed her sister on the forehead, and whispered some encouragement. But Lizzie lay still on the couch, unmoved. The police then escorted Lizzie to the jail in Taunton. Outside the police station, Rufus Hilliard granted an exclusive interview to Henry Trickey of the *Boston Globe*. "In the performance of my duty," he said, "I have been called upon to arrest the daughter of a man whose family I knew and respected and whose life I knew nothing against." The crime's horrific implications greatly disturbed him, he said. All murders were terrible, but this crime defied understanding. It was incomprehensible that a woman who had led such an exemplary life could murder her parents. The "charge becomes greater," he claimed, "than that of common murder and the gravity of the situation is appalling." Because of the family's prominence, the police had worked diligently to avoid any misstep. They had exhausted every clue "that would turn suspicion away from the daughter." After hours of thoughtful consideration, Hilliard and Knowlton decided that the evidence was strong enough to warrant an arrest.

The public formed their own opinions about Lizzie's guilt or innocence. Newspapers published opinions and theories of all kinds, and letters poured into Knowlton's office, running the gamut from confessions to unsolicited theories on the actual killer and motives.

One anonymous writer condemned Knowlton and the police for their unscrupulous tactics that trampled the "rights of a noble woman." The critic accused Knowlton and his "tools" of bungling the investigation and of targeting "an innocent young lady, whose character and virtue are as much above yours as the light and sky of day are above the darkness." Another writer denounced Lizzie as a "double murderer" who had brutally chopped up "those two poor old people, all for money and spite and hate." The writer declared that Lizzie was the Devil's child and that she had hired an "unprincipled lawyer to get her off." If the district attorney didn't do his duty, "she will chop up someone else." The writer hoped the hangman would hang Lizzie twice to avenge the two brutal deaths.

A written confession arrived from Philip Gordon Reid in Albany, New York, who claimed that he was Andrew Borden's illegitimate son. Reid said that Borden, to cover up his sins, sent the boy's mother to an insane asylum, where she died from a broken heart. Reid was placed in a New York orphanage and then indentured to a farmer. After he reached maturity, he said, he went to Borden to demand a fair share of the man's fortune. Although Borden agreed to pay him off, Abby Borden blocked the deal. Reid was furious not just because Borden reneged but because Mrs. Borden had once insulted his mother. He vowed right then to avenge the insult as well as Borden's betrayal. He confessed that he murdered the couple at eleven forty-five in the morning on August 4, 1892, and dropped the hatchet from a steamer at the Fall River dock. Reid wrote that "Miss Lizzie Borden my half-sister may have heard of me," and now "to shield her father's infamy and good name," she was stoically and nobly "taking the course" of the law. After mailing the letter, Reid boarded a train to parts unknown. He clearly never meant to surrender, and the police never followed up, dismissing him as a crackpot.

Knowlton received unsolicited help from spiritualists. A self-proclaimed trance medium and physician, Dr. J. Burns Strand, wrote Knowlton that he had had a vision in his sleep. He heard a voice tell him that the assassin murdered the woman first with a hatchet or knife. Channeling Borden, the spirit told Strand that "some of my Daughters [are] plotting with Uncle Morse and a strange man. Oh, my daughters did this." Strand offered to help Knowlton solve the crime—for a price—but Knowlton refused.

While letters from crackpots flooded Knowlton's office, Lizzie's women friends publicly rallied behind her. The Women's Christian Temperance Union held a meeting at Boston's Tremont Temple on Sunday, September 4, 1892, to petition the governor for bail. According to the *Fall River Daily Globe*, there was no precedent for bail for "a person charged with murder under these circumstances." Appealing to the audience's maternal instincts, Susan Fessenden, the president of the Women's Christian Temperance Union, reminded them of Lizzie's exemplary service to numerous Christian organizations, including the Christian Endeavor Society. She referred to Lizzie as a "poor orphan" and asked the women in attendance to do their Christian duty and sign a petition for bail.

Not everyone agreed or even sympathized. The *Fall River Daily Globe* criticized the Women's Christian Temperance Union for using its Sunday meeting as a blatant emotional appeal to influence the judicial process. Although the *Globe* agreed that everyone had a right to an opinion, it criticized the meeting as "ill-timed and in extremely poor taste." The newspaper accused the women of using sentiment to manipulate the public—and predicted that ultimately judge, jury, and the rule of law would prevail over maudlin female sentiment.

As reporters dug into the story, it soon became apparent that the Borden household was far from harmonious. Although many people conceded that Borden was an "honest" businessman, no one characterized him as a loving and devoted father or husband or compassionate friend.

ᛏ ᛏ ᛏ

BORDEN'S ANCESTORS HAD LIVED by their own rules and often clashed with authority. John Borden arrived in Boston in 1635 from Kent in

England. He was allegedly banished to Portsmouth, Rhode Island, along with Anne Hutchinson for heresy in 1638. Anne Hutchinson was a religious "free thinker" who challenged male church authority with her unique interpretation of scripture. John Borden's son John, born in 1640, was jailed in 1684 for refusing to pay his property taxes. He eventually owned all the land known as the West End of Fall River. His son Richard purchased water rights and additional land in present-day Fall River to resolve a land dispute. By 1714 Richard and his brother owned virtually all of Fall River and much of what is now Swansea and Somerset. Richard's son, also named Richard, was born in 1750. Over the years, the Borden family amassed a considerable fortune, but in one generation it disappeared. Richard's son, Abraham, Andrew's father and Lizzie's grandfather, lacked the family's business sense and quickly lost the family fortune. When he died, he left his son, Andrew, the water rights and the family homestead at 12 Ferry Street—which was nothing more than a slum cottage.

Through perseverance and hard work, Andrew Borden vowed to restore his family's fortune. But his business tactics contradicted his reputation for honesty. He began his career as the sole agent for Crane's Patent Casket Burial Cases, offering a money-back guarantee on his superior caskets. If the coffins were too small for the deceased client, he would just cut the feet off the body and stuff the truncated corpse into the box. Borden subsequently began to purchase commercial properties that he rented to new businessmen. He monitored the businesses carefully and as soon as they turned a profit, Borden raised rents. He also purchased foreclosed farm property and resold it at a considerable profit.

In April 1844, Borden started an undertaking business with William J. Almy at the corner of South Main and Anawan streets in Fall River. With the two men's industry, the business thrived. Borden and Almy retired from the business in 1878, although they continued in real estate. Rumor had it that Almy "became mentally deranged" after retirement. An anonymous "graybeard" at the cemetery on the day of the Borden funeral thought that Almy's and Borden's violent deaths were the consequence of their dishonesty and greed. The partners often swindled clients, selling them expensive caskets and then switching them with cheaper ones at burial.

*Fall River, a thriving mill town in 1892. Andrew Borden was an influential presence throughout the community, with blocks and buildings bearing his name. (Fall River Historical Society)*

In 1845, Andrew met Sarah Morse, a farm girl. They married the same year, on December 16. According to his friends, it was a love match that produced three children. Emma was born March 1, 1851, and Alice Esther was born in 1856 but died two years later. When Lizzie was born, on July 19, 1860, Andrew was disappointed that she was not a boy. Thinking he would never have a male-heir, he christened his daughter Lizzie Andrew Borden.

In 1863, Sarah Borden died at the age of 40 from "uterine congestion" and spinal disease. Lizzie was not yet three. Two years later, needing someone to manage his daughters and his house, Andrew married Abby Durfee Gray, whose father sold tin from a pushcart in Fall River. Abby was thirty-eight and had never been married.

Borden paid his debts promptly and showed no mercy to those who didn't. He was equally parsimonious in his personal life, denying himself any sensual pleasure. He was active in the Congregational Church's temperance movement. He not only abstained from alcohol, but despised those who indulged. Some temperance advocates also advised against the use of "excitants" or spices in food, as they might stimulate a desire for alcohol. The Borden breakfast of cold mutton, left-over soup, and johnnycakes exemplified the temperance mindset. A typical breakfast, in 1876, included beefsteak, bacon, eggs, fried potatoes, wheat cakes, sausage, porridge, doughnuts, and fruit.

Some people may have admired these stingy traits, but to the *Providence Journal* they were signs of false piety and a mean spirit. The cold mutton typified "fittingly enough the whole character of the murdered man." His refusal to fit in with the "smart set" or his inability to "cut a dash" were positive traits in themselves, but not in the extreme. Borden's miserliness was as sordid as unbridled extravagance. In hoarding money, Borden "forfeited the natural privileges" of his hard work. He ignored his obligations to his family in depriving them of the benefits that accompany wealth.

Borden "loved money more than he did his children," the *Journal* claimed. Those people who "can afford to live well and who live meanly, usually think meanly and act meanly"—and perhaps die meanly. It is no wonder that Andrew Borden's funeral drew thousands of spectators but few genuine mourners.

# CHAPTER THREE

# Press Coverage—
# Sensation, Hype, and Hoax

The press uniformly portrayed Andrew Borden as a miserly tyrant, but the image of Lizzie Borden varied depending on the source. An anonymous letter to the *Fall River Daily Herald* argued that Lizzie's behavior was suspicious and unfeminine. The writer stated that 999 women out of a thousand would have behaved much differently after discovering the mutilated corpse of their dead father. Most women would have screamed or even swooned. Lizzie, however, had calmly walked to the back stairs and called to Maggie to go for a doctor. Numerous critics attributed her lack of emotion to mental derangement. A prosecuting official who wished to remain anonymous told the *Fall River Daily Globe* that Lizzie's "eyes and movements, her physical makeup and mannerisms" were consistent with mania. If Lizzie was not insane, then the crime was even more horrible.

Officer Philip Harrington thought Lizzie's behavior was odd also. When he questioned her just after the murders, "Lizzie stood by the foot of the bed and talked in the most calm and collected manner," according to his preliminary witness statement. She never expressed any "sign of sorrow or grief, no lamentation of the heart, no comment on the horror of the crime, and no expression of a wish that the criminal be caught." Harrington suspected that this "very peculiar woman" knew more than she said. "I don't like that girl," he told the marshal. "Under the circumstances she does not act in a manner to suit me; it is strange, to say the least."

Lizzie's behavior after the murder did not surprise her uncle, Hiram Harrington. After all, he stated in the *Fall River Daily Herald*, "Lizzie is of a repellent nature." Now Emma, Harrington said, was a different story. Quiet and unassuming, Emma had always exhibited traditional feminine traits and emotions, but not Lizzie. Her uncle described Lizzie as "haughty and domineering with the stubborn will of her father."

Was Lizzie really an unfeminine creature capable of the unthinkable? Her friends met with a *Boston Globe* reporter to argue otherwise. They discussed Lizzie's modesty and her dedication to the church, saying that "in Lizzie Borden's life, there is not one unmaidenly nor a single deliberately unkind act."

According to her friends, Lizzie was very shy, and this shyness had prevented her from making friends, even in childhood. Although she was not academically gifted, she had received high rankings at the Morgan Street Elementary School because of her perseverance and hard work. In high school, she studied piano but abandoned it because she failed to master the instrument, and she dropped out of high school after a year because "it was not congenial to her tastes." After she left school, Lizzie and Emma lived quietly at home with their parents. Neither displayed any professional ambition or any inclination toward marriage. Emma was satisfied to live demurely with her parents as a devoted daughter. Lizzie was drawn to the church and regularly attended services at the local Congregational church. She also enjoyed dancing and the theater.

Lizzie's shyness made her awkward socially. At first, churchwomen misinterpreted her shyness as haughtiness and avoided her. In 1887, however, a woman from the church encouraged her to participate in the church more actively, and Lizzie made a profession of faith and embraced the denomination's high ideals. She became more open and receptive to others but also put aside frivolous activities, including dancing and the theater. "I have been so long doing nothing in this world," she said, "that I shall have to make up now for the delinquency." She also joined the Young Women's Christian Temperance Society in its campaign against intemperance. She taught for awhile in a missionary school for immigrant mill workers, but teaching didn't suit her. She realized that her talents were more artistic than pedagogical and devoted her energies to decorating the church and organizing entertainment that Congregationalists approved.

A trip to Europe in 1890 introduced Lizzie to a more sophisticated world, far beyond the limits of her father's home and the provincial Fall River community. She gravitated to the art museums and to Old World architecture and sent home photographs and copies of great masterpieces. The trip awakened a previously dormant aspect of Lizzie's nature. After she returned to Fall River, she regaled her friends with long, entertaining descriptions of her travels. She was a witty, engaging raconteur, her friends said; she was certainly not aloof and austere, as reported in some newspapers. In fact, she had an excellent sense of humor and loved a good joke. Although she refused the romantic advances of eligible young men, she nonetheless enjoyed their company. One friend referred to Lizzie as "a thoroughly womanly woman" with an eye for beauty and appreciation for literature, ranging from Dickens to Carlyle and Emerson. She was a complex woman, her friends said, who had "too much gentle forbearance" to harbor any hatred or murderous thoughts.

After her friends began to defend her, Lizzie stepped forward and granted an interview with Kate Swan McGuirk of the *New York Recorder*. Lizzie denied the charge that she was an unnatural, cold woman; it was inappropriate, she thought, to express private emotions in public. "They don't see me cry," she said. "They should see me when I am alone or sometimes with my friends." Looking into Kate's eyes, Lizzie said, "I have tried hard to be brave and womanly through all this." The press had criticized her for not wearing appropriate mourning dress, but Lizzie pointed out that her father had disdained the practice, and she was merely respecting his preferences.

Julia Hayes Percy of the *New York Herald* attributed Lizzie's reserved behavior to her "gentle breeding," comparing her to a "thoroughbred." She likened Lizzie to the innocent and aristocratic French women who calmly went with dignity to the guillotine during the Reign of Terror. Percy accused the "big brawny policemen" of not properly respecting Miss Borden's station. They had casually referred to the Borden sisters by "the easy use of Christian names, which is somewhat startling to the casual listener," but these same policemen politely referred to "the housemaid as Miss Sullivan." This practice implied a reverse class bias against Lizzie.

In October, a new story in the *Boston Globe* presented a more sinister portrait of Lizzie, a portrait that fed into the public's more dire suspicions. On October 10, 1892, a front-page headline read, "Lizzie Had a Secret. Mr. Borden Discovers It, Then a Quarrel." Crime reporter Henry Trickey promised to reveal the "real" Lizzie.

His story consisted of testimony that Edwin McHenry, a private investigator, had taken for the government's case. The story painted a sordid picture of a manipulative Lizzie who had few redeeming qualities. It also "revealed" that Lizzie had had a secret affair with her uncle, John Morse, that she had played a role in the 1891 robbery of her house, and that she had had a long-simmering hatred for her stepmother.

In one of these troubling eyewitness accounts, Mrs. Gustave F. Ronald, who said she was staying at the Wilbur Hotel on the day of the murder, told McHenry that she was strolling down Second Street with her child. When she approached what she learned later was the Borden house, she said, "I suddenly heard an awful cry or moan, coming from someone apparently in terrible pain." She looked in the direction of the sound, up toward the second floor of 92 Second Street. "I saw a woman," she said, "with what I would call a rubber cap, such as women use when cleaning house." This strange woman looked out at the street, but when she saw Mrs. Ronald she slammed the window shut and disappeared. Curious about the murder, Mrs. Ronald went to the inquest and immediately recognized the woman who had been at the window: it was Lizzie.

The affidavit from the Chace family was even more shocking. The Bordens had invited the Chaces to visit after supper on August 3, the night before the murder. When they arrived, Mrs. Chace overheard a heated argument between Andrew and Lizzie. "You can make your own choice and do it tonight. Either let us know what his name is, or take the door on Saturday, and when you go fishing, fish for some other place to live, as I will never listen to you again. I will know the name of the man who got you into trouble."

As the guests continued to the dining room, they heard Lizzie say, "If I marry this man, will you be satisfied that everything will be kept

# Globe.

DAILY GLOBE:
Sept. '92 - - 200,143
Sept. '91 - - - - - - -154,178
GAIN - - - 45,965

—TEN PAGES.　　　　　　　PRICE TWO CENTS.

on Main st., a man rushed out on to the sidewalk, having a GLOBE above his head, and shouted:
"For heaven's sake have you seen THE GLOBE?"
The headlines were soon seen, and then there was a furious rush for the news stand. Men trampled on each other in their eagerness to secure a paper, and in a short time the sidewalk was crowded with an excited mob, reading the startling news.
It fairly electrified the crowd.
Meantime a boy fought his way through the crowd and put a flaming bulletin out upon the sidewalk. The crowd became denser and denser, and excitement raged. Passers by stopped, read and dove into the news depot, some returning with two or three papers. Three men stood behind the counter working to satisfy the demand for GLOBES. Men threw down their money, grabbed the paper and became absorbed in the story without waiting for their change. Some could not contain themselves, and fairly shouted in amazement as they read.
Boys with huge bundles were rushing about Main st., shouting, and together with

**The Excited Readers**

made the centre of Fall River a regular pandemonium.
Inside of 10 minutes several thousand people were gathered about Main st., from Pleasant to Franklin sts., reading and discussing.
And still the demand for GLOBES had not been half met.
There were corner gatherings and animated discussions, but not the expression of diverse opinions.
Mingling among the crowd THE GLOBE correspondent heard such expressions from many lips as this: "This is a sad day for Lizzie Borden. I had asked myself what could have incited her to do it, if she did it, but there is no doubt about a motive now. It is all explained.
"I had hoped she might be proven innocent, but it looks hard for her now, and her past life—why, great Scott. Fall River never knew her, her intimate friends did not know her."
No story ever caused such a furor, because none ever came with such corroboration or so unexpectedly.
Boys carried GLOBES into the mills, where they were eagerly read by the operatives while they tried to work.
Detective McHenry's spying upon Lizzie in some quarters met with condemnation, but it was quickly supported by many who cry: "If the woman is guilty she deserves conviction; any method to serve the ends of justice is right."
THE GLOBE'S story caused an awful cloud to settle over the influential part of the city. On the hill, among Lizzie Borden's friends, and around the Central Congregational church, there was a gloom that was pathetic. In that part of the city hopes in her innocence were centred, hopes that aroused to fervent prayer. The GLOBES went there, they were read, but it was a grave matter for them. No outburst of excitement appeared in this quarter, but there was a poignant grief. Many went for Lizzie Borden, whom hope had buoyed up for weeks. She was their fellow church member, their friend in many

# LIZZIE HAD A SECRET.

## Mr. Borden Discovered It, Then a Quarrel.

## Startling Testimony of 25 New Witnesses.

## Seen in Mother's Room With a Hood on Her Head.

## Accused Sister of Treachery and Kicked Her in Anger.

## Theft of a Watch---Money Offered to Bridget ---Story of a Will.

FALL RIVER, Mass., Oct. 9.—Besides those who testified for the government in the preliminary examination of Lizzie A. Borden before Judge Blaisdell fully 25 new witnesses will be called by the State at the trial of the defendant for murder in December.
On the afternoon of September 1 Miss Borden was committed to the county jail at Taunton to await the action of the grand jury at its November sitting.
Judge Blaisdell's jurisdiction not being final his action in thus concluding the examination was justified in two ways. He knew that if he dismissed the defendant she would soon be under arrest on a bench

one in which he saw Miss Lizzie is so situated that she must have been standing

**Over the Mutilated Remains**

of her mother at the very time that her father was about to enter the house, between 10.30 and 10.45 o'clock.
The next witness of importance is Mrs. Gustave F. Ronald, whose husband is a well known civil engineer, and whose home during the winter is at Pawtuxet, R. I.
She and her husband were guests at the Wilbur House at the time of the murder.
About 9.30 o'clock on the morning of Aug. 4 she went out with her baby in its carriage for a walk.
She wheeled the little one on 2d st. and

Sensationalist exposé of the Borden tragedy in the October 10, 1892, Boston Globe. The article marked a sad day for the Globe, however; within hours of publication, the story fell apart as a hoax. (Boston Public Library) from the outside world?" Lizzie angrily walked past the Chaces, who heard Abby Borden say to her husband, "You must not get so angry with Lizzie, as she has a terrible temper, and there is no telling what she might do to herself."

Andrew Borden was uncharacteristically open with the Chaces, telling them he "would rather see her dead than have this come out." He had implied that Lizzie had become pregnant and that her own uncle, John Morse, had seduced her.

According to Trickey, Maggie Sullivan told McHenry that quarrels were nothing unusual in the Borden household. In fact, the night before the murder, she had overheard Morse advise Lizzie to stop the quarreling because it would only lead to more trouble. He told her that "something else has to be done and he would help if he could."

Further, McHenry reported, Maggie said that after the murders Lizzie had offered her money to keep quiet. Maggie had been so frightened that she spent the night at Dr. Bowen's.

Trickey's article reported that Detective McHenry had gone to great lengths to spy on Lizzie while she was in the Taunton jail, waiting to testify at the inquest. First he had hidden under the bed in the matron's room, and then hid behind a curtain. He could see and hear Lizzie and visitors. At one point, he said, he was "within 17 feet of Lizzie Borden when he saw Lizzie kick Emma three times." She "threw a biscuit at her and called her a 'd—- b——.'" Lizzie accused her sister of giving her away so she could inherit all the money. McHenry thought Lizzie "was almost insane in her manner at the time."

To many people, this sordid *Globe* story confirmed Lizzie's guilt. Following the *Globe's* lead, the *Boston Evening Record* compared Lizzie to the legendary Lucrezia Borgia, "a woman of a strange, unaccountable type, a woman whose very coldness of exterior was cloak for the fiercest passion." The *Globe*, through Trickey's reporting and McHenry's investigation, had seemingly solved the enigma of Lizzie Borden. She was a "peculiar" woman whose transgressions included sins other than murder. The righteous churchgoer who had taught mill workers was nothing more than a promiscuous, thieving woman who hacked up her parents and then threatened the maid to keep quiet!

The sensational *Globe* story turned out to be an elaborate hoax. No sooner had the exposé hit the streets than it unraveled. Although the names sounded familiar, no one had bothered to check the facts, identify the witnesses, or verify addresses. According to Lizzie's attorney, Andrew Jennings, it was a "tissue of lies," a humbug, part Gothic thriller, part potboiler. In fact, most of the people mentioned did not even exist; those who did vehemently denied the statements. No one with the surname Ronald had stayed at the Wilbur Hotel on the days mentioned in the article. No one named Frederick Chace lived in Fall River. In fact, the Chaces' alleged address, 198 Fourth Street, did not exist.

The next day, the *Globe* published a front-page retraction, in which the editors apologized to Miss Borden "for the inhuman reflection upon her honor as a woman."

Neither Trickey nor McHenry fared well after the scandal. Knowlton indicted Trickey for fraud, and both the *Globe* and John Morse threatened lawsuits. McHenry closed his Providence office and moved to Albany; Trickey fled. On December 5, 1892, while boarding a train in Ottawa, Canada, he accidentally fell to his death.

While Trickey, McHenry, and their story were completely discredited, the rumors and speculations about Lizzie's guilt did not abate entirely.

# CHAPTER FOUR

# The Trial

Over the next few months, Lizzie sat in her cell reading, visiting with family and friends, and arranging interviews. The grand jury officially indicted Lizzie on December 2, 1892. Jennings rejected any insanity defense, convinced that his client was not insane. The *Fall River Daily Globe* reported that Lizzie had spent a "cheerless" Christmas, without friends or gifts. Mrs. Livermore remained active on Lizzie's behalf. She accused the government of violating Lizzie's constitutional rights to a swift and speedy trial. The press attributed Mrs. Livermore's nagging letters as the defense's attempt "to break down the government's case." About a month before the trial, Mrs. Livermore arranged an interview for Lizzie with Amy Robsart of the *Boston Post*. However when Amy and Mrs. Livermore arrived, Lizzie agreed to meet only with Mrs. Livermore.

Livermore talked with Amy Robsart on the train back to Boston. Mrs. Livermore described Lizzie, now thirty-three, as refined and intelligent but not pretty. When she asked Lizzie about her stolid indifference, which disturbed the public, she responded, "What would they have me do? Howl? Go into hysterics?" Lizzie asked how anyone could think her guilty. Why commit "a crime like that in broad daylight, with the certainty of detection, with people going to and fro on the street with Maggie washing windows and likely to come in for water at any minute?" If Lizzie wanted to kill her father and stepmother, why not wait until they slept? She could have removed her bloody clothes and gone to bed, no one the wiser.

▼ ▼ ▼

IN JUNE 1893, NEW BEDFORD geared up for one of the most celebrated trials in New England history. Lawyers, reporters, and spectators flooded the city and crowded the hotels. The Parker House, the largest hotel in the city, was booked to capacity. The management set aside nine rooms for jurors and additional ones for the sheriff; out-of-town press used the hotel as their headquarters.

Several female journalists, including Elizabeth Jordan of the *New York World*, Kate McGuirk of the *New York Herald*, and Amy Robsart of the *Boston Post* covered the trial from a woman's perspective. Robsart's reports captured the odd mixture of Sunday go-to-meeting and carnival atmosphere that pervaded New Bedford. Newspaper men smoked, gossiped, and watched the church folk. As the Salvation Army marched by singing "I'm on My Way to Jesus," Robsart wrote, one "sacrilegious wag intimated that if they were no further on their way than New Bedford, they'd probably never get there."

On Monday, June 5, the trial began in unrelenting heat. As spectators gathered on the courthouse steps, the attorneys took their places in the courtroom. The imposingly rotund District Attorney Hosea Knowlton and his younger associate, William Moody, represented the prosecution. The clean-shaven Andrew Jennings, Melvin Ohio Adams ("with a humorous twinkle in his eye"), and ex-governor George Dexter Robinson (with "spectacles firmly set astride his nose") stood for the defense. Emma and Lizzie had hired Robinson two months earlier because he was an experienced and savvy trial attorney. He was a skilled and popular politician who had served the Republican Party well in the U.S. House of Representatives and Senate; he had also served as governor of Massachusetts from 1883 to 1886.

The sheriff had designated four tables up front for the press. Julian Ralph, of the *New York Sun*, sat in the New York "annex," "serious eyed and getting bald." In the front row sat Joseph Howard, a New York columnist famous for his coverage of high-profile trials. The *Boston Globe*, perhaps to restore its reputation after the Trickey fiasco, had engaged the renowned Howard to cover Lizzie's trial.

Howard wrote that no one yet knew much about the circumstances of the case except that Lizzie and Maggie had been the only people in the house at the time of the murder, other than the victims. The family quarrels and Lizzie's "unnatural reserve of bearing and coldness of demeanor" certainly did not indicate guilt. Howard concluded that the evidence was circumstantial at best. He predicted that the Borden trial would either fall apart because of the lack of convincing evidence "or it will be the most complete vindication of the potency of circumstantial evidence ever known."

By ten fifty-five, everyone had taken seats. Robsart observed that the courtroom was filled with "a flower garden of hats and rainbow of feminine finery." One young woman kept her opera glasses trained on Lizzie throughout the trial. While some of the women spectators were intelligent and refined, many were hardened women who "gloated over the more repulsive details in the testimony." Workmen in shirtsleeves and women in modest calico gowns filled the room.

After the attorneys and judges settled in, "the heroine of the day" arrived, dressed fashionably in a black merino dress, and a hat and gloves. Reporter Joseph Howard corrected the popular misperception about Lizzie's physical appearance. Although many people thought she was an "Amazon," in actuality she was a well-proportioned and self-possessed woman of medium height. Her eyes had an unpleasant stare, he said, full cheeks, and an "obstinate and stubborn chin." Amy Robsart described her as "well figured" with prominent deep blue eyes. Her face was broad and her hair was swept upward into a fashionable French twist. To Robsart, "she looked incapable of crime."

During jury selection, Judge Albert Mason dismissed a number of potential jurors who opposed the death penalty, and finally he impaneled twelve men representing an interesting cross-section of Bristol County. The jury included Frank Cole, a jeweler; John Finn, a painter; Lemuel Wilbur, a farmer; and the foreman, Charles Richards, a real estate man and local politician.

Lizzie remained stoic throughout the first day of the proceedings, often wiping the perspiration from her face and vigorously fanning

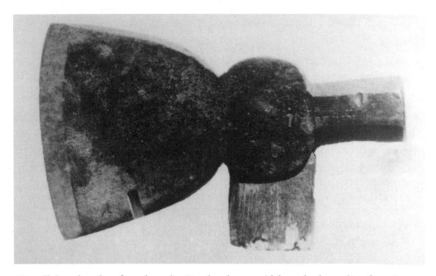

*Handleless hatchet found at the Borden home. Although the police found several axes, including this one, they never recovered the actual murder weapon. (Fall River Historical Society)*

herself. She spoke only once, when asked to enter her plea. In Howard's words, she "obeyed the mandate with a frigidity that ought to have cooled the entire atmosphere" while pleading not guilty.

The next day, June 6, another hot day, the actual arguments in the trial began. William Moody opened for the prosecution. His opening focused primarily on Lizzie's relationship with her stepmother, arguing that it was contentious at best. Lizzie was angry because of a property dispute five years earlier. Moody based his argument on Lizzie's visit to Miss Russell's house the previous night in which she "was predicting disaster and cataloguing defenses," and her unkind reference to Mrs. Borden as a "mean thing." He also pointed to Lizzie's visit to Smith's Drug Store to purchase prussic acid, a deadly poison. Soon after that, the Mr. and Mrs. Borden fell ill.

Moody also presented as proof Lizzie's conflicting statements about her visits to the barn and contends that Lizzie fabricated the alleged note from a sick friend. Lizzie had also lied about her whereabouts when her father returned from downtown. He told the jury that Lizzie was upstairs and "at that time, gentlemen, Mrs. Borden's body lay within plain view of that hall, dead, probably more than an hour." He then moved to Lizzie's behavior immediately after discovering her father's body. Lizzie walked through the sitting room "without stopping to look at her dead father, upstairs by the room where her stepmother lay dead, without an inquiry, without a thought."

Moody then introduced the "hatchet theory." One of the axes the police retrieved had what the police thought were blood spots and hair strands. Holding the hatchets found in the investigation, Moody admitted that "upon careful examination neither of these hatchets seem to contain the slightest evidence of bloodstain." He then refers to "another weapon or part of a weapon," the handleless hatchet. At some point, the handle had broken off the hatchet in some violent act. The hatchet blade was covered with ashes and rust. He told the jury that Dr. Wood would testify that someone could have successfully washed off blood after the murder. He stated that the measurement of the wound on Mr. Borden's skulls conformed to the "exact measurement of the blade of that hatchet." The fact that the killer did not drop the weapon beside the victim indicates that the murderer was "familiar" with the "house's resources for destruction, obliteration, and concealment."

Furthermore, Lizzie's decision to burn the dress also indicates guilt. Moody argues that Lizzie's motive was her growing hatred for her stepmother, but he fails to present motive for Andrew's murder.

At one point, when he brandished the victims' preserved skulls, Lizzie was so overcome that she "dropped her head and gently slid from her upright position." It took more than thirty seconds for the "not over-bright deputy sheriff" to discover that she had fainted. As Andrew Jennings administered smelling salts and the deputy fanned Lizzie, others crowded around her, blocking her from much-needed air.

Joseph Howard christened the third day, June 7, as "woman's day" because of Maggie Sullivan's testimony and the usual coterie of women among the courtroom spectators. "New Bedford's fattest and leanest of the feminine gender" pressed so hard to get inside the courthouse that the police joined hands to prevent a stampede through the barrier. As the women crowded into the courtroom, one woman bragged that she had farmed her children out to various relatives and left her "old man to prepare his own breakfast." The cloying odor of stale food, fennel seed, and flowers that graced the judge's bench, along with the heat and humidity, created an unpleasant and stifling environment.

John Walsh, the police photographer, testified that morning regarding the crime scene and post-mortem photos. As Moody questioned Walsh, the photographer introduced the corresponding photos. Exhibit Nineteen graphically depicted Borden's mutilated head and unrecognizable features. He also showed photographs of Abby's body on the floor beside the dresser and a close-up of her head that graphically detailed the numerous wounds.

In the afternoon, Maggie Sullivan took the stand; Howard said her testimony was a "sensation." During the testimony, Lizzie "changed her seat," according to Howard, "so that she could look the witness full in the face, exerting, it was thought, a more or less magnetic influence on the woman." Maggie provided valuable insights into the family. When asked about breakfast, Maggie told the court that "there were some mutton, some broth and johnnycakes, coffee, and cookies." After the Bordens and Mr. Morse finished eating, Maggie prepared to wash the windows. She said that Mr. Morse left at about eight-fifty and Lizzie came downstairs shortly before nine o'clock. She asked Lizzie if she wanted any breakfast, but she said she did not feel well enough to eat.

At that time, Mr. Borden was in the sitting room reading the paper and Mrs. Borden was dusting in the dining room. At some point, Borden left to run errands downtown. Maggie spent the next couple of hours washing the windows. Shortly before ten-thirty, she went into the sitting room to clean the windows from the inside. She heard something that attracted her attention.

"Will you describe what you heard which attracted your attention?" Moody asked.

"Well, I heard like a person at the door was trying to unlock the door and push it but could not, so I went to the front door and unlocked it."

"What did you do with the reference to the lock with the key?"

"I unlocked it. As I unlocked it, I said, 'Oh, pshaw,' and Miss Lizzie laughed, upstairs—her father was out there on the doorstep. She was upstairs."

"Upstairs; could you tell whereabouts upstairs she was when she laughed?"

"Well, she must be either in the entry or in the top of the stairs, I can't tell which."

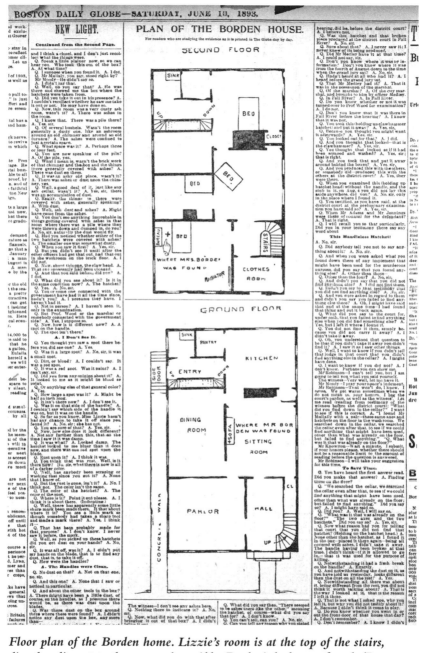

Floor plan of the Borden home. Lizzie's room is at the top of the stairs, directly adjacent to the room where Abby Borden's body was found. (Boston Public Library)

Borden proceeded to the sitting room when Lizzie came down-stairs and asked her father about the mail. She then asked Maggie if she was going out in the afternoon. Maggie said, "I don't know; I might and I might not; I don't feel very well." Lizzie then said, "If you go out, be sure and lock the door, for Mrs. Borden has gone out on a sick call, and I might go out, too." Maggie asked, "Miss Lizzie, who is sick?" Lizzie answered that she didn't know.

Maggie then told the court that after she finished her chores, she went to her room to rest at approximately eleven o'clock. The next thing, she heard Lizzie call for her and she rushed down the back stairs. She saw Lizzie with her back to the screen door. When Maggie started for the sitting room, Lizzie stopped her, "Oh, Maggie, don't go in. I have to have a doctor quick. Go over. I have to have the doctor." Lizzie then told Maggie that "I was in the back yard and heard a groan, and came in and the screen door was wide open." She then asked Maggie to go for Miss Russell, "Go and get her. I can't be alone in the house."

Maggie ran over to Dr. Bowen's house but he was out and then went to Miss Russell's. When she returned to the house, she found Mrs. Churchill and Dr. Bowen, who walked out of the sitting room and said, "He is murdered; he is murdered." The door to the sitting room had been open before the murder.

"What happened then?" Moody asked.

" 'Oh,' I says. 'Lizzie, if I knew where Mrs. Whitehead [Abby's half-sister] was, I would go and see if Mrs. Borden was there and tell her that Mr. Borden was very sick.' She says, 'Maggie. I am almost positive I heard her coming in. Won't you go upstairs to see.' I said, 'I am not going upstairs alone.' "

Mrs. Churchill accompanied Maggie up the front steps. Maggie said, "As I went upstairs, I saw the body under the bed. I ran right into the room and stood at the foot of the bed."

Moody asked, "Was the door leading into that chamber where Mrs. Borden was found dead open or closed as you came up the stairway?"

"Open," she answered.

Maggie and Mrs. Churchill then returned to the dining room. Lizzie was lying on the dining room lounge with Miss Russell. Maggie then told Moody that she knew nothing about a note from a sick friend or about any hatchets.

On cross-examination, Robinson asked about the family relationships.

"It was a pleasant family to be in?" he asked.

"I don't know how the family was; I got along all right."

"Never saw the least, — any quarreling or anything of that kind?"

"No, sir, I did not."

Robinson then turned to Maggie's inquest testimony.

"Did you in answer to this question, 'Did they talk pleasantly?' say 'Yes, sir.' And 'they talked over things at Christmas, and if anything was the matter with Mrs. Borden, Lizzie did all she could for her.'"

"I did not know what the matter was between them."

"Didn't you testify that?"

"I don't remember anybody asking me such a question."

"You said, 'They seem to get along congenially.'"

"Yes, sir, for all I saw."

Robinson then focused on the time Borden returned from running his errands.

"After you let Mr. Borden in, you say you heard Miss Lizzie laugh?"

"Yes, sir."

"And you say she was upstairs somewhere?"

"Yes, sir."

"And you didn't see her on the stairs?"

"No, sir."

As Maggie's testimony grew to a close, Robinson challenged her memory.

"Well, a good many things that day aren't very clear in your mind. Are they clear in your recollection?"

"As far as I remember; as far as I know."

Throughout the long ordeal, Howard said that she told the story of the murders "straight as a string."

On the fourth day, June 8, the crowd piled into the courtroom to hear some of the most explosive and anticipated testimony. In the afternoon, the prosecution called Alice Russell, Lizzie's longtime friend and confidante who now testified for the prosecution. She told the court that Lizzie had visited her the night before the tragedy and had expressed a sense of foreboding. She said that the family had been violently ill and that she feared something dreadful might happen. She was frightened that someone would burn the house down, especially since her father was discourteous to so many people, including Dr. Bowen. "I feel something is hanging over me," Lizzie told Alice. "I cannot tell what it is." After Alice arrived at the Borden's house after the murder, she decided to stay until Sunday to assist Emma and Lizzie.

Moody then directed Alice's attention to the dress-burning incident. Alice told the court that on Sunday, August 7, three days after the murders, she found Lizzie in the kitchen standing near the stove, holding a skirt that was "covered with paint." Lizzie told Alice that she was "going to burn this old thing up; it is covered with paint." Further, she said, she had seen Lizzie either ripping something down or tearing a part of this garment. However, Alice never witnessed Lizzie burning the dress. On Monday, Alice told Lizzie, "I am afraid, Lizzie, the worst thing you could have done was to burn that dress. I have been asked about your dresses." Lizzie then said, "Oh, what made you let me do it? Why didn't you tell me?" On cross-examination, however, Alice confirmed that Lizzie had ironed handkerchiefs the morning of the murder. Robinson then asked if Alice had seen any blood on Lizzie's clothing, face, or hands. No, she had not.

Alice also testified that Lizzie and Emma had cooperated with the police, who had thoroughly searched Lizzie's and Emma's rooms. Alice stated that the police had "full sway" of the house, but she was not present during the actual search.

On the fifth day of the trial, Friday, June 9, the temperature had dropped to a comfortable level. Officer Philip "Natty" Harrington, who had questioned Lizzie right after the murders, took the stand. He had a remarkable memory for colors and images, from the blood that ran down Borden's face to the style of Lizzie's dress that day. He testified that when he arrived at the Borden house around twelve-thirty, he saw Borden's body covered with a sheet. Harrington said that Borden's "face was all cut and covered with blood. The clothes were stained, the shirt front and part of the coat." Harrington then went upstairs and saw Mrs. Borden's body. He "noticed that the head had been cut and there was blood around the floor, blood on the back of the dress." He saw blood spots on the pillow sham and the spread. When he left the room, he saw Lizzie standing in her room at the foot of her bed. Harrington described her as "cool" and unemotional. She told him that she was in the barn when her father was murdered. When asked about any possible suspects, she said that her father had argued with a disgruntled tenant. Harrington then said that "owing to the atrociousness of the crime perhaps you were not in the mental condition to give as clear a statement of the facts as you will be tomorrow." She assured him she was, stiffly curtsied and left.

$$\Upsilon \quad \Upsilon \quad \Upsilon$$

HARRINGTON AND OTHER OFFICERS searched the house and barn. Moody asked Harrington about the conditions in the barn a few hours after the murder. First he asked about temperature in the loft.

"As to degrees, I cannot say, but it was extremely hot," Harrington answered.

"Did you notice anything as to dust at that time?"

"Yes, sir, it was very dusty, very uninviting, the floor, bench, and hay, an old fashioned fireplace, which stood in the north-west corner of the barn, and some window screening and binding cords—things that were covered with dust."

Harrington then testified that the windows were closed, "covered with cobwebs" and clothes. While searching the barn, the officers pitched the hay, which stirred up a considerable amount of dust. Harrington noted that the air was "suffocating." On cross-examination, Harrington faltered. When Robinson asked about the curtain on the barn window, Harrington could not remember distinctly if the curtain had been rolled up or if it had yellowed. When asked if the window was open or shut, Harrington answered that the window was "not opened, when we entered." Robinson then directed his attention to his testimony at the inquest. He had testified that the door on the yard level was open. He recanted this testimony, stating that it was incorrect.

"Is that the way you testified before?" Robinson asked.

"Well, you say it is there, but the door was shut, sir."

Harrington also stated that the "window on the west was open" not closed as he had testified earlier. He remembered that the officers opened the window during the search because of the heat.

On Saturday morning, June 10, the sixth day, the crowds waited outside the courthouse as usual for Lizzie's arrival. A large group of giggling schoolgirls arrived, less interested in the trial than in posing for the photographers. Those spectators who were denied access found other diversions. While the prominent members of the prestigious Wamsutta Club—none under the age of 80—played croquet, others searched for "Howard's cow" that had mooed almost on cue throughout the trial.

In the morning, Officer Francis L. Edson testified that on Friday morning, August 5, he took several axes from the cellar. On cross-examination, Robinson challenged police competence and asked Edson if he "did not see any slighting of the work by any of them?" Edson denied any incompetence.

On cross-examination, Robinson asked what specific area Edson searched. He answered that he searched the boxes near the chimney that contained ashes and cinders. Robinson then questioned Edson's thoroughness.

"You were very thorough about your work."

"What I done."

"Didn't anything escape you, Captain?"

"Might have been."

Robinson asked if other officers were competent and Edson answered yes. He then asked if anyone else took anything from the house on Monday. Edson answered that "Officer Medley had a hatchet head in his pocket" wrapped in paper.

"It was only the small hatchet—had no handle?" Robinson asked.

"No handle."

Edson then told Robinson that he did not put the axes in a bag, but carried them "openly" in his hands.

Officer Dennis Desmond wrapped it in paper and took it to the city marshall's office. It was covered with "dark spots here that resembled blood on the blade." It was unclear if the stains were rust or blood.

Officer William Medley confirmed Harrington's earlier testimony that that the barn loft was extremely hot and dusty. He testified that nothing had been disturbed and that the windows were closed.

He further testified that on Monday when the police searched the cellar, he found a small hatchet blade in a box, but no handle. This "handleless hatchet" was in a box with other rubbish. Moody showed him the hatchet head and he identified it as the one he found. The head was "all covered with dust, and there were some dark spots here that resembled blood on the blade." Coarse dust covered the entire blade. He reported his findings to Desmond, wrapped the hatchet in newspaper, and took it to Marshal Hilliard at the police station.

Officer George Seaver testified that he and other officers searched the house thoroughly and saw numerous blood spots where the victims had been killed. He testified that on Saturday, August 6, he found the handleless hatchet in a box in the cellar. He showed it to Officer John Fleet and they then returned it to the box. The defense implied that if Edson and the other officers had searched the cellar as completely as they testified, why didn't they discover the blade sooner? Unlike Phil Harrington, Seaver had little knowledge of women's style and could not distinguish a challie from a delaine. He did recall that he gave a black silk dress to Mr. Fleet, who closely examined for blood but found none. Seaver saw no blood on any of the dresses, including a blue one.

⊤　⊤　⊤

AT NOON, THE COURT RECESSED for the rest of the weekend. The Wamsutta Club members dropped their croquet mallets and everyone ran back to the courthouse. All eyes were riveted on the door, waiting for Lizzie. As she emerged, in her high-buttoned dress, hat, and gloves, she descended the steps alone as a man held the screen door open. She looked pensive and introspective, her eyes directed downward.

When the trial resumed on Monday, June 12, the heat was once again oppressive. While others looked refreshed, Howard thought that Lizzie's "color was bad, her manner listless, and it seemed as though the demon of apprehension was dallying with her sensibilities." Once again, "a swollen crowd of female idlers" packed the courtroom. The onlookers seemed eager to learn if the court would allow Hosea Knowlton to introduce Lizzie's inquest testimony into the official record. Lizzie's lawyers wanted to exclude the testimony because they claimed Knowlton had taken unfair advantage of Lizzie, ordering her to appear without counsel at the inquest shortly after the murders, when her nerves were still frayed. They argued that Knowlton's frequent badgering had confused Lizzie so much that she often contradicted herself. When the chief justice ruled to exclude the inquest testimony, Lizzie broke down in tears. Elizabeth Jordan of the *New York World* wrote that Lizzie cried not from joy but because she "was touched by the fairness and justice of the decision."

Onlookers reacted according to their own biases. "That is logic and good law," said one. "The Commonwealth would have been disgraced by any other decision." "Great God!" said another, "it is a crying shame that justice should be defeated and a murderer protected because of so slight a point as that decision is based on."

On Tuesday, June 13, the eighth day, there were serious questions about courtroom procedure. The prosecution was scheduled to introduce what proved to be its most "carnal house performance" as the medical experts testified in excruciating detail. The defense was concerned about its possible effect on Lizzie, who had collapsed once before, when she saw her parents' skulls. Her lawyers and "church friends" greeted her warmly, while Joe Howard noted that a number of the spectators stared at her "as though she were a beast."

Knowlton's first witness, medical examiner William Dolan, described the "sickening scene" better than any "magic lantern." At one point, Knowlton asked him about "a dress waist, a dress skirt, and under white skirt." Dolan first saw these items during the house search the Saturday after the murder. Knowlton showed Dolan the blue dress and white skirt.

"Were those the articles that were handed to you by Mr. Jennings?"

"That is the dress and skirt."

Dolan examined the articles and stated that "there is a minute pin spot of blood on the skirt. I cannot find it now." At one point, Dolan, to demonstrate the position of the body, placed Andrew Borden's coat on a chair and then a plaster cast of Borden's head on top. He then described in great detail the location of wounds on the skull and in graphic detail the assassin's blows to the head. When asked about the hatchets, Dolan testified that he had examined the claw hammer under a magnifying glass. He found two hairs on the blade and on the wood that he gave to Professor Wood. When asked about the handleless hatchet, he said that he had nothing to do with it.

Lizzie sat motionless throughout the testimony. "Was ever a girl, a child of tender training, placed in such a position? Guilty as Judas or spotless as Cordelia, what torture must she have suffered!" Julian Ralph wrote in the *New York Sun*. Lizzie demonstrated the "ideal American nerve." Occasionally she shielded her face behind the fan, but for the most part she fixed her eyes on the witness.

Although Lizzie withstood the testimony well, Ralph reported that the "diabolic word painting and parade of sanguinary exhibits" caused one juror, Louis Hodges, to faint. Despite all his analysis, Dolan testified that he could not pinpoint the exact cause or even time of death.

The next witness was a chemist, Professor Edward S. Wood from Harvard University Medical School, who presented more evidence about blood and hair. When asked about the hair found on one of the axes, Wood answered:

"The envelope marked 'Hair taken from the hatchet' contained when I opened it two pieces of paper, this one, which was sealed and which contained a short hair." The envelope was now empty, but his examination revealed that the hair was "unlike human hair, and it had a red brown pigment, and is more similar to a cow's hair than any other animal whose hair I have ever examined." He further concluded, "it is animal hair, there is no question of that, and probably cow hair." This was the only hair, he stated "which I have had as coming from the hatchet."

Knowlton asked about the contents of the victims' stomachs. Wood answered that he tested the contents for prussic acid, but found none or any poisonous substance.

On cross-examination, Melvin Adams asked about the handleless hatchet and the presence of rust. He asked that if the hatchet had fallen into damp ashes, would the appearance "be consistent with what you saw upon the face of this hatchet, namely as dust adherent to its surface?"

"Yes, sir, if the ashes were damp."

Thus, the spots found could be rust and not blood.

Adams then asked about the spot of blood on the white skirt.

"Are you able to say that that was not a spot of blood which might have gotton on from the menstrual flow of a woman?"

"No, sir, I am not."

"It would be entirely consistent with that, would it?"

"Yes, sir, it may have been menstrual blood, or may not, as far as I can determine."

On re-cross, Wood testified that the blood spatter from the victims would have covered the murderer. Earlier testimony determined that no one saw blood anywhere on Lizzie's face, hands, or clothes.

Howard concluded that the prosecution had yet to present any convincing evidence against Lizzie.

The weather was more oppressive the next day. A heavy rain had fallen, but it had done nothing to cool the temperature. Lizzie and the jury suffered the most, as they were confined in cramped quarters. Lizzie's face was swollen from crying; once again, she appeared "limp and without energy." Even the jury seemed tired. Mrs. Hannah Reagan, the jail matron, was called to testify about the conversation she had overheard when Emma was visiting Lizzie in jail on August 24. She stated that she hard Lizzie say, "Emma, you have given me away, haven't you?" Emma said, "No, Lizzie, I have not." During cross-examination, Mrs. Reagan was often defiant and flustered. She could not remember the date, the time, or the names of visitors, yet she could recall specific conversations. She forgot the time of Emma's second visit because she said the earlier quarrel between the two in the morning had flustered her. However, she proudly remembered her bet with Lizzie about the proper way to break an egg. Jennings called her attention to the paper that Mr. Buck asked her to sign in which she denied that any such argument occurred. She refused under Marshal Hilliard's orders.

The next morning Lizzie entered the courtroom carrying a colorful bouquet. Her demeanor suddenly changed when several women lovingly surrounded her, "laughing and chatting for several minutes in conversation cheerily participated in by Lizzie herself." When the court threw out the testimony about prussic acid, Lizzie thankfully opened her eyes and smelled the blossoms. Eli Bence had testified that Lizzie had visited Smith's Drug Store and asked to purchase prussic acid. He refused because it was a deadly poison that required a doctor's prescription. Suddenly her face flushed with color and she laughed with her attorneys.

At ten-thirty on the morning of Thursday, June 15, District Attorney Knowlton rested his case. In Howard's opinion, he had not made his case; he had not been successful at connecting "the prisoner with ax, hatchet, blood, or anything whatever, save an unmotivated opportunity to kill her stepmother." Knowlton had based his case primarily on Lizzie's hatred for her stepmother. Lizzie had fabricated the note from Mrs. Borden's sick friend and had lied about the visit to the barn. After the dinner break, Emma appeared for the first time and greeted her sister affectionately.

That afternoon, Andrew Jennings rose to open for the defense. Julian Ralph compared him to a medieval knight who eloquently did battle for his client. His tone was "low, measured, and funereal" with a "touch of melancholy." For his part, Joseph Howard said Jennings had an "admirable voice" that he used effectively.

Jennings began by talking about his years of personal service to the Borden family. He had known Lizzie since childhood and emphasized her exemplary character and devotion to the church. He reminded the jury that the prosecution had not introduced any direct evidence that connected Lizzie to a weapon or to the murderous act. The prosecution's case, Jennings argued, was solely based on circumstantial evidence. The government argued motive, weapon, exclusive opportunity, and the defendant's conduct and appearance. Jennings criticized the government's argument that who killed the stepmother then killed the father. However, the prosecution presented no motive for Andrew's murder.

Jennings then turned to the alleged weapon. The blood that was allegedly on the ax "has disappeared like mist in the morning." Furthermore, the claw-head hatchet that Dr. Dolan was certain killed Andrew had also disappeared. Jennings stated that the prosecution must produce the actual weapon and then connect it with the crime or provide a logical reason for its disappearance. The prosecution had failed to do this.

One of the prosecution's expert witnesses, Professor Wood, testified "that there was no blood anywhere on anything."

Jennings then turned to exclusive opportunity. The defense would argue that because of the amount of street traffic, any number of people could have entered the Borden house and committed the murders.

Jennings would also disprove the prosecution's argument about the dress burning. Evidence would prove that the dress was covered with paint, not blood, and that Lizzie burned the garment "in the broad light of day in the presence of witnesses, with windows open, with the inside door open, with officers on every side of the house." Furthermore, she willingly gave the police the navy blue silk dress that she wore that morning.

Jennings concluded, reminding the jury about the presumption of innocence. The defense would prove that Lizzie had no motive to murder her parents, that no one found any blood evidence on her person, and that a witness would confirm her alibi about the barn.

The defense team opened with several witnesses who supported this theory.

Some had seen strangers in the neighborhood. Mark Chase stated that at about eleven o'clock in the morning on August 4, he saw a man dressed in a "brown hat and black coat" sitting in a carriage that stood "right by a tree in front of Mr. Borden's fence." He had never seen the man before and thought it odd that the carriage sat in front of the Borden house for so long. On cross-examination, Knowlton failed to rattle the witness into contradicting his testimony.

In addition to Chase's man in the carriage, Dr. Benjamin Handy testified about the "strange man" he had seen. As he drove by the Borden house sometime between ten-twenty and ten-forty on August 4, he saw a man lurking around the house. The man was acting more strangely than anyone Handy ever seen before: "He seemed to be either agitated or extremely weak, staggering, or confused, or something of the kind."

The defense introduced testimony that confirmed Lizzie's alibi. Ice cream peddler Hymon Lubinsky testified that when he drove past the Borden house a few minutes after eleven o'clock, he "saw a lady come out the way from the barn right to the stairs from the back of the house." He said the lady was wearing a dark dress and later identified her as Lizzie.

When the session resumed in the afternoon, two "clever and amusing little witnesses" provided some much-needed comic relief: Everett "Brownie" Brown and Thomas Barlow, both about 15. They both testified that they were just "knocking around" and happened by the Borden house a little after eleven on the morning of August 4. Brown testified, and Barlow later corroborated, that the two had gone into the allegedly hot barn shortly after the murder.

According to Barlow, "me and Brownie" returned to the Borden barn later because they said it was actually cooler there than outside, in spite of the sloping roof and closed window. Knowlton was puzzled, as Officer Philip Harrington and other witnesses had testified that the barn was hot and suffocating.

"And you should think the barn loft was cooler than any place you found that day?" Knowlton asked Barlow.

"Yes, sir."

"You mean that, do you?"

"Yes, sir."

"Has anybody told you to say that?" Knowlton asked.

"No sir."

"Have you talked with anybody about this case?"

"Nobody but Mr. Jennings."

"Anybody else?" Knowlton asked. "When did you talk with him?"

"I can't say now; some time last week."

"It really struck you as being a cool place, up in the barn?"

"Yes, sir."

"A nice, comfortable, cool place?"

"Yes sir."

Knowlton was suggesting that Jennings had coached the impressionable young witnesses to discredit the police testimony about the stifling conditions in the barn.

On June 16, Jennings called John J. Manning, a reporter for the *Fall River Daily Herald*. When he arrived at the Borden house sometime after eleven-thirty, he went upstairs with Office Doherty and saw Mrs. Borden's corpse. He helped to pull the bed away to facilitate the investigation. He described her body and the blood spots at the scene.

When asked about his involvement with Mrs. Reagan and the alleged argument between Emma and Lizzie, he said that Mrs. Reagan told him "that there was nothing" to the story. On redirect, Manning testified that Mrs. Reagan knew he was a local reporter with the Associated Press. He had gone with a colleague, Mr. White of the *New York World,* to check the validity of her story.

Thomas told the court that he had walked into Mrs. Reagan's room and said, "I see you are getting yourself into the papers, Mrs. Reagan." She laughed and said yes, but "they have got to take that all back." She then denied the story about the argument between Emma and Lizzie.

Marianna Holmes testified to Lizzie's character and the events after the murder. Howard described her as a "nice little old lady with a large face and large voice." She emphasized Lizzie's strong moral character, her devotion to the church, and her missionary work with the Christian Endeavor Society. When Mrs. Holmes spoke at length about the church organizations, Knowlton objected. She bristled and curtly said, "Excuse me, I am not used to such business, and I expect to overlap."

Mrs. Holmes had been in the Borden home the morning of the funeral and had been with Lizzie when she went into the room with the caskets.

Jennings asked, "What did Lizzie do?"

Before Mrs. Holmes answered, the court gave her a chair and Lizzie buried her face in her handkerchief. Mrs. Holmes said that "Lizzie shed tears over the casket" and kissed her father.

ᚭ ᚭ ᚭ

ON THE AFTERNOON OF THE ELEVENTH DAY of the trial, June 16, Emma Borden took the stand with self-reliance and dignity. Julian Ralph described her as "the typical old school marm"; Joseph Howard wrote that "there was no swaying of her slender form, no drooping of her straight-out eye, no quivering of her tight-shut mouth." Emma's testimony about the burned dress discredited Alice Russell's earlier testimony and allayed suspicion that Lizzie had burned it to hide evidence. Emma said that Lizzie had worn the cheap dress to help paint the house the month before the murders. (A later witness, house painter John Grouard, corroborated her story.) Because it was so severely stained and faded, Alice had asked Lizzie why she hadn't burned it yet. According to Emma, after Lizzie destroyed the dress, Alice told her that it was the worst thing she could have done. "Why then did you let me do it?" Lizzie asked.

Knowlton then cross-examined Emma. With his forceful personality making him seem, to Julian Ralph, the "personification of the inexorable spirit of the law," he asked Emma about the burned dress.

Knowlton turned to family relationships.

"Do you still say that the relations between your sister and your mother were cordial?"

"The last two or three years they were very."

Knowlton then pressed Emma about her inquest testimony.

"Now I want to ask you if you didn't say this: 'Were the relations between you and your stepmother cordial?' Answer: 'I don't know how to answer that. We always spoke'"?

"That was myself and my stepmother."

"How does it happen that you remember the answer in which you did not explicitly state whether they were cordial or not, but don't remember an answer, if one was given, in which you said they were not cordial, which was the following question?"

"I don't understand."

The court then recessed. During the recess, Mary Livermore (Lizzie's mother's friend) sat down beside Lizzie, and the two kissed affectionately. Not one to discourage publicity, Mrs. Livermore granted an interview to the *Boston Journal*. She told the reporter that she had just returned from Chicago's World's Fair and had hurried to the trial to support Lizzie. In her view, the trial was going "triumphantly," as the prosecution did not have "the slightest possible fact to rest upon." She also explained that "it is always our practice . . . to burn up everything that is of no value, so as to get the useless things out of the house." In fact, Emma had told her that she and Lizzie often burned unwanted items. "They were people who did not want clutter around." Mrs. Livermore was convinced that the defense would win an acquittal.

WHEN EMMA RETURNED TO THE STAND, Knowlton asked her about Miss Russell's testimony about the dress burning. He asked if the testimony was truthful. Emma answered that it didn't seem so, because she didn't remember it. She further denied asking Lizzie what she planned to do with the dress.

Knowlton turned to the alleged argument in the matron's room. Emma emphatically denied any such altercation.

"Now, Miss Emma, on that morning did you have any conversation with Miss Lizzie in which she said, 'Emma, you have given me away, haven't you?'"

"I did not."

"And did you say in reply, 'No, Lizzie, I haven't.' 'You have,' she says, 'and I will let you see I won't give in one inch.' Was there any such talk as that?"

"There was not," Emma answered.

"Was there ever any trouble in the matron's room between you and your sister while she was there?"

"There was not."

"Any quarrel of any kind?"

"No, sir."

Again, Knowlton failed to rattle her.

The court adjourned until Monday, June 19, at nine o'clock. Church bells rang out on Sunday, June 18, calling parishioners to worship. Jurors were obligated to attend services. After church, Deputy Sheriff Nickerson purchased a box of cigars for the jury, and the jury took a barge ride where "the fumes of those 5-cent cigars arose and floated and gracefully disappeared." While the jurors enjoyed their cigars and Lizzie sat in her cell reading Dickens, Justice Justin Dewey sat on a rock at Clark's Point breathing in the cool ocean air. The preoccupied Knowlton walked from his office, while ex-governor Robinson "dashed" and "flitted" from breakfast to supper, contemplating his closing argument. Defense attorney Melvin Adams lingered at the supper table enjoying "the good things of this life to eat and drink." The weekend over, on Monday, June 19, Robinson and Knowlton made their final arguments. Her face swollen, Lizzie entered the room carrying a red-and-white carnation.

Governor Robinson, dressed in a black suit and alpaca coat and wearing half-glasses, rose and spoke in a "low, earnest tone" as he recalled the murder. Robinson stated that the prosecution had built its weak case on the "hatchet theory" and "exclusive opportunity theory" as well as the alleged bad blood between Lizzie and her parents. Robinson argued that these theories were seriously flawed. He also accused the police of targeting Lizzie from the beginning and dismissing other possible suspects.

The prosecution had argued exclusive opportunity—that Lizzie was in the house alone with her parents and had every opportunity to commit the crime. Robinson pointed out that Lizzie had every right to be in the house: after all, she lived there. Her activities in the house were not unusual. She was performing domestic chores that were common in American households. He reminded the jury that Maggie had unlatched the side door, giving numerous people access. The defense had presented several witnesses who testified that they saw several people lurking around the house who could have slipped into the side door undetected. So much for exclusive opportunity.

Robinson also challenged the prosecution regarding the note from the sick friend that Mrs. Borden told Lizzie she received. Simply because no one had acknowledged sending the note did not mean it didn't exist. Robinson argued that the author might not have come forward because of an aversion to publicity and to public appearances in court.

The prosecution had argued that Lizzie's failure to discover Mrs. Borden's body when she took her laundry upstairs also indicated her guilt. Quite the contrary. Robinson reminded the jury that the guest room door was closed and that Lizzie had no reason to enter the room.

Robinson next addressed the prosecution's challenge of Lizzie's alibi, her visit to the barn. The police concluded that Lizzie had lied because they found no footprints on the dusty floor. Robinson reminded the jury, however, that the police had compromised their own investigation. Several people, including the police officers and "me and Brownie," had traipsed around the loft, making it virtually impossible to distinguish one set of footprints from another. Furthermore, the ice cream peddler Lubinsky testified that he saw Lizzie leave the barn around eleven o'clock.

Robinson also challenged the theory that Lizzie had burned the old dress to destroy blood evidence. Lizzie had worn the dress in question in May to help paint the house and it was thus covered with paint. It was customary practice in New England homes to burn ruined clothing. Furthermore, she burned the dress not in secret but when the police were on the premises. Burning the dress was nothing more than a common domestic practice and certainly not an attempt to cover up a crime. The police had found a small bloodstain on one of Lizzie's skirts; it turned out to be menstrual blood.

The prosecution and the press had focused on the contentious family relationship. Robinson argued that the relationships in the Borden household were no more factious than in any other New England household. Andrew Borden, who was a plain, unostentatious man, wore one piece of jewelry—a ring that had belonged to Lizzie, which he never removed. The ring, Robinson argued, symbolized the close father-daughter bond, a bond that endured even in death. "No man should be heard to say that she murdered the man that so loved her," Robinson said. He also referred to Lizzie's statement about Abby: "She is not my mother. She is my stepmother." Whereas the prosecution interpreted that statement negatively, Lizzie had only been stating a fact that reflected her longing for her own mother, not hatred for Abby.

Robinson argued that the prosecution's hatchet theory was equally unconvincing. The officers could not agree which hatchet they discovered in the cellar was the murder weapon. Robinson referred to the handless hatchet that the prosecution theorizes "did the business." The government's theory was that the murderer used the hatchet to kill the Bordens and then promptly washed off the blood. The murderer then broke off the handle. Even though the handle was broken off, there was a small piece of wood in the eye of the hatchet. Professor Wood testified that blood could have flowed into that narrow space. He discovered no blood on the hatchet. Furthermore, the government admitted that that hatchet may not have been the weapon. The prosecution is "trying a case of may-have-beens." Furthermore, none of the blades conforms to the wounds. When a person strikes its target with the hatchet and then pulls out the weapon, the size of the wound is broader than the blade. Then how could the police explain the cuts that did not fit the dimension of any of the hatchets?

As Robinson closed, he reminded the jury that it was virtually impossible for Lizzie to commit both crimes within the time frame. How could she possibly have murdered her stepmother, changed her clothes, gone into the cellar to wash off the blood and then returned upstairs? If she had changed the first time, Maggie would have noticed it. Then after she killed her father, she would once again have had to change, wash off the blood down in the cellar, wash off the hatchet, break the handle, and then throw the blade in the box of cinders—all this within fifteen minutes. Robinson contended that this was virtually impossible.

Finally, the crime was simply out of Lizzie's character. Her demeanor and conduct throughout the trial spoke to her innocence. He reminded the jury that a mistaken verdict was irreparable. If the jury had any reasonable doubt, it must acquit. "Take care of her," he concluded, " . . . and give us promptly your verdict 'not guilty' that she may go home and be Lizzie Borden of Fall River in that bloodstained and wrecked home where she has passed her life so many years."

Howard was disappointed with Robinson's closing. "It fell far short of the anticipation in both matter and manner," he wrote. Ralph agreed and thought that Robinson presented it with the "wrong spirit" and that it never touched the jury's heart. The *Boston Post*, however, applauded Robinson's closing as "a masterpiece of argument" because it was "an appeal to common sense." He spoke plainly without flourish or overly dramatic rhetoric, the *Post* reporter believed. After Robinson closed, it was Hosea Knowlton's turn. He forcefully threw himself into the prosecution's closing argument. He moved quickly around the courtroom, making sweeping gestures and looking from the jury to the prisoner and then to the spectators, who crowded forward. His elaborate rhetoric included rhetorical flourishes and literary allusions to Shakespeare's *Lady Macbeth* and Dickens's *Bleak House*.

In Knowlton's version of the murders, Abby Borden, not her husband, was the primary target. Lizzie's negative statement that Abby was not her mother revealed Lizzie's deep-seated hatred that gnawed at her and drove her to commit the unthinkable. Although Lizzie's stepmother, Abby had assumed the mother's role when Lizzie was only five years old. Since then, she had nurtured her in illness, encouraged her, and genuinely loved her as if she were her natural daughter. When Andrew Borden gave his wife a small piece of property, however, Lizzie reacted with petty jealousy and turned on the only mother she had known. Knowlton argued that Lizzie's refusal to call Abby "Mother" was as deep a cut as any hatchet blow.

At this point, the court adjourned until the next day. On June 20, Knowlton rose to continue his closing. According to Knowlton, Lizzie was a calculating woman who had planned the murder meticulously. She had even set the stage with her visit to Alice Russell by planting the seeds of premonition so that when the tragedy occurred the prophecy was fulfilled. Knowlton established the theory of exclusive opportunity, in that Lizzie was alone with the victims at the time of the murder. After she checked on Maggie's whereabouts, she followed Abby upstairs to the guest room and murdered her. She then waited in the room for her father to return. She walked downstairs and "transformed from the daughter, transformed from the ties of affection, to the most consummate criminal we have read of in all our history or work of fiction." Still wearing the blue Bedford cord murder dress and carrying the ax, she attacked her father to hide her earlier crime. During the violent act, the handle broke. She discarded the handle, probably in the kitchen stove, and then hid the claw head in the cellar. "Crime breeds crime, and it is the mother of crime," Knowlton argued.

Knowlton argued that Lizzie's visit to the barn was a smoke screen. He emphasized the inhospitable environment—the dust, the heat—and discredited those "wonderful boy detectives" "me and Brownie" because their testimony did not conform to the experience of others in the barn. Furthermore, Lizzie chose that very moment to visit the barn at the specific moment an assassin murdered her father.

Lizzie's behavior immediately after discovering the body was equally suspicious, Knowlton averred. He compared her reactions to those of Charles Sawyer, the civilian who was commandeered to guard the door. Like any normal person, Sawyer quickly locked the cellar door, frightened—even though a strong man—that the murderer was still on the premises. If Lizzie was innocent, why did she stay in the house? Wouldn't an innocent person escape as quickly as possible to avoid becoming the next victim?

Knowlton discounted the defense's theory about the burned dress. Lizzie did not destroy it, as Robinson alleged, because it was stained with paint but because it was drenched with the victims' blood. Knowlton insisted that Lizzie had lied about what dress she wore that day. Knowlton argued that Lizzie was wearing the Bedford cord, not the navy blue silk dress, when she murdered her parents. After the murders, she hid the dress. During the police search, she gave the police officers the navy blue silk afternoon dress that she claimed she was wearing that morning—the same dress she wore while ironing handkerchiefs. What woman, Knowlton asked, would wear a silk afternoon dress to do household chores on a hot summer day? He argued that Lizzie hid the dress until Sunday morning, when she burned it in the stove not to discard a useless paint-stained garment, but to destroy incriminating evidence—the life blood of her now dead parents.

Knowlton concluded that Lizzie lied about her alibi, constantly contradicted herself, and fraudulently gave the police the wrong dress. Having heard the evidence, the jury now had to decide whether that evidence was credible. He further cautioned the jurors against allowing a misguided sense of mercy to interfere with their duty. "Rise, gentlemen, rise to the altitude of your duty. Act as you would be reported to act when you stand before the Great White Throne at the last day," Knowlton said. If the jury hears "the voice of his inner consciousness" he will hear God's voice say, "Well done, good and faithful servant" and can then "enter into the reward" of "eternal life." Knowlton concluded his long argument at five minutes past twelve.

Lizzie, according to Joseph Howard, kept her eyes riveted on Knowlton and "lost no word, no inflection, no gesture but looked at him as though with a pitying amazement at the whole procedure." Howard compared Lizzie to a "suspected witch" who had been tied at the stake with cords "that had cut into her flesh and spirits for ten months." She sat through Knowlton's closing argument without flinching. After Knowlton completed his closing on June 20, Judge Dewey began delivering the charge to the jury at one-forty-five. He spoke for ninety minutes. The spectators were riveted; Lizzie leaned forward and listened with "breathless anxiety." Dewey praised Lizzie's Christian character, criticized the police for carrying their search too far, and challenged the prosecution's exclusive-opportunity theory. The jury could not pronounce the defendant guilty based on circumstantial evidence, unless they were convinced beyond a reasonable doubt. During the trial, the judge had disallowed two pieces of possibly incriminating evidence: Lizzie's inquest testimony and the prussic acid testimony.

When Dewey finished, the jury retired to deliberate. A mere thirty-five minutes (and one ballot) later, they had a decision. (According to Juror Lemuel K. Wilbur, the jurors had made up their minds even before the closing statements.) Foreman Richards suggested that they wait an hour for the sake of appearance. Shortly after four-thirty, the twelve men returned to the courtroom. As they filed into the box, all looked directly at Lizzie.

As Lizzie stood up, Julian Ralph noted that "there was such a gentle, kindly light beaming in every eye that no one questioned the verdict that was to be uttered." When the foreman announced, "Not guilty!" Lizzie collapsed against the rail, the courtroom erupted in cheers, and crowds of well-wishers rushed toward her. Even the judges responded with uncharacteristic emotion.

Andrew Jennings hurried to his client's side and raised her head. Knowlton, the "stern old head," ignored Lizzie and walked over to

Governor Robinson to congratulate him. Robinson then rushed to Lizzie, put his arm around her, and gently lifted her up. As the attorneys supported her, her friends broke rank and rushed to congratulate her. After the excitement subsided, the jurors filed past Lizzie. She smiled at them, warmly shook hands, and expressed her gratitude.

Lizzie asked Governor Robinson to remain after the courtroom emptied. He was the surrogate father whose support for her had never wavered. From the beginning, he had been one of the few men who steadfastly believed in her innocence and in his ability to win an acquittal. Before he accepted a retainer, Robinson had insisted on talking with Lizzie, hearing her voice, and looking her in the eye. He went to the Taunton jail with Andrew Jennings and Melvin Adams and spent two hours alone with Lizzie. Afterward, he told the other lawyers, "She is innocent. I am ready to stand by her." According to the *Boston Herald*, Robinson said that Lizzie was "not only a true lady, but as amiable, tender, and kindly a woman who our ladies have to be." According to the reporter, Robinson "restored her natural self" because for six months she had been alone with everyone against her. After Knowlton "bullyragged" her at the inquest, she thought "he was all powerful" and that he would twist the facts against her. Robinson dispelled her fears. He "came to her like rain upon a desert" and his "absolute faith in her" restored her.

Lizzie soon learned that the verdict had stunned many Fall River residents who did not share New Bedford's joy in her acquittal. Her attorneys feared that hostile crowds would gather at the Second Street house, so they urged her to spend the night with Marianna Holmes and her husband in their Fall River home, some distance from the Borden house.

After the verdict, several hundred people had gathered around the courthouse. As the bloody exhibits, including the sofa, were carried out the back door and put into a cart, Lizzie walked out the front door a free woman, to the accolades of a cheering crowd. Within minutes, Lizzie climbed into a carriage for a reception of well-wishers at the Holmes residence. At the house, Emma sat in a plush armchair while Lizzie, still wearing black, relaxed opposite her. According to a *Boston Herald* reporter, Lizzie's demeanor had changed for the better; she showed no sign of the anxiety or strain of the past year. Her eyes had brightened, and an animated joy replaced the stoicism. As she walked into the dining room, she said, "Well, you ought to let me do just as I please." As friends continued to arrive for a supper party, disappointed crowds at the Second Street house dispersed.

After Lizzie and Emma left the courthouse, the jurors went promptly to City Hall to collect their wages and pose for photographs. They then headed for the Parker House for the "source of consolation so lovingly denied them, where they drank to Lizzie Borden's health and their own."

In his final article in the *Boston Globe,* Joe Howard wrote that Lizzie reacted to the verdict as he had expected—with quiet dignity. An ordinary woman might have expressed more emotion, but Lizzie was "a puzzle psychologic." She had coped by shutting herself off from the onslaught of mean-spirited onlookers and turncoat friends.

T    T    T

LIZZIE RETURNED TO 92 SECOND STREET the morning after the verdict. What were her thoughts when she finally returned to the house for the first time in a year? What did she think when she saw the empty spot where the sofa had been? When she walked up the front stairs to her room, did she stop momentarily at the guest room door? Or did she quickly retreat to her room? The house was now empty, except for her sister, Emma. Maggie, who had no desire to return to work for the Bordens, now worked for Joshua Hunt, the jail keep in New Bedford. Emma and Lizzie were now alone in the house, alone with their thoughts and perhaps alone with the truth.

# CHAPTER FIVE

# The Aftermath

I f Lizzie Borden wasn't the one who "took an ax," who was? Was it the disgruntled tenant who wanted to open a rum shop? Or was it Dr. Handy's "madman" who had been skulking around Second Street? Other rumors circulated. During Lizzie's trial, Jose Correiro, a Portuguese farmhand, killed Bertha Manchester at her Fall River farm with an ax and then left her on the floor in a position similar to Mrs. Borden's. While the press noted some similarity, the police saw it as coincidence. Other rumors suggested that Maggie Sullivan knew the burglars who had robbed the Borden house the year before the murders. Was one of them Maggie's gentleman friend? The robbers knew the house well, so perhaps Maggie had let them in to finish the job. Some rumors even pointed to Dr. Seabury Bowen because there had been bad blood over money between him and Andrew Borden.

Lizzie's acquittal had not allayed the public's fears. A murderer still walked the streets of Fall River. Every year on or around August 4, for fifteen years, the *Fall River Daily Globe* reminded the readers that "The Thing" was still free. The editor attributed supernatural powers to this creature, envisioning it walking through locked doors and waiting to murder again. Because the crime remained unsolved, the *Daily Globe* called on the police to reexamine the list of Borden's enemies: mill managers, farm hands, and tenants. If this investigation failed, then the mad man still walked the streets.

In 1898 the editor noted that many infamous murderers had since been tried and executed, but the Fall River "Thing" remained at large. During the Spanish American War, the editor made the improbable claim that The Thing was Captain Valeriano Weyler, the ex-captain general of Cuba, who had mercilessly killed a half million Cubans. The theory quickly fizzled; Weyler had never been in Fall River.

The *Fall River Daily Globe* ended these editorials in 1907, having failed to develop any plausible theory. The police never arrested anyone else for the Bordens' murder; in fact, according to the *Daily Globe*, the police would say that the only suspect "is not five minutes travel from a police station"—that is, at Lizzie Borden's house.

The press followed Lizzie's movements after the trial and conjectured about her and her sister's decision to remain in Fall River. Shortly after the verdict, the sisters purchased a large thirteen-room Victorian on Fall River's fashionable "Hill" at 306 French Street with the money they had inherited from their father. The new house, Maplecroft, was a far cry from the old tenement house on Second Street. Equipped with four bathrooms and a modern kitchen, it was Lizzie's showplace; she elaborately decorated it with silk drapes and mother-of-pearl light fixtures.

Lizzie reinvented herself after the trial. She changed her name to Lizbeth. She became an active patron of the arts, a society matron, and an animal advocate. She attended church only once; after sanctimonious churchwomen pulled their skirts away from her in disgust, she never returned. In June 1894, Lizzie evicted the Young Women's Christian Temperance Union from the Borden building, reportedly because of the women's stinging insults.

Scandal continued to dog Lizzie. The *Providence Journal* reported that in February 1897 she allegedly stole two paintings from the Tilden-Thurber art gallery in Providence. The Providence police never issued a warrant, and the gallery refused comment. Lizzie was also involved in a scandalous relationship with the actress Nance O'Neil.

While the once-supportive church abandoned Lizzie, Mary Livermore remained a loyal companion and often attended the theater with her in Boston. Lizzie even tried her hand at playwriting, but apparently never published anything.

Over the years, Emma and Lizzie grew apart, perhaps over money, perhaps over Lizzie's choice of friends. Emma vehemently disapproved of the lavish theater parties at Maplecroft and of Lizzie's unseemly friendship with the actress Nance O'Neil. The critics described Nance as "a real woman" with thick brown eyebrows, small mouth, and hands that "crumble like rose leaves in her grasp." Lizzie first saw Nance when she appeared as Lady Macbeth in 1904 at the Colonial Theater in Boston and was immediately enchanted. She showered the actress with gifts and paid her legal expenses in a lawsuit against a Boston theater manager. The unconventional relationship deeply offended Emma. Lizzie also threw lavish parties that might have included liquor. By 1909, the friendship had ended, perhaps because of Nance's escalating financial problems or because of Lizzie's past.

Edwin J. Maguire of the *Boston Sunday Post* tried again and again to arrange an interview with Lizzie, but she vehemently refused. When he visited Maplecroft, he noticed that the staff had drawn the shades and bolted the heavy oak doors. He repeatedly rang the bells and knocked on the doors, but no one answered. "The caller might well have tried to gain response from a tomb." He telephoned, but Lizzie told him that she had "nothing, absolutely nothing to say" and slammed down the receiver. She had become more reclusive because of the public's animosity, due probably to what Maguire called her "phlegmatic, impassive temperament." After her relationship with Nance ended, Lizzie became even more reclusive.

Emma Borden, however, did agree to an interview, to correct the lingering suspicions. In April 1913, she met with Maguire at her new home. (In 1905, she had moved in with the family of the late Reverend Edwin Buck.) Emma was a "gentle-mannered woman" with a "pink and white complexion that a debutante might envy." Her eyes "seemed to reflect the sorrow and grief that were part of the heritage she received through the untimely death of her father."

Emma told Maguire that "the tragedy seems but yesterday" and like a "frightful dream." She often wondered why the police had never arrested anyone else. She responded to the charge that Lizzie acted queerly. Who hadn't done something peculiar at times? she asked. "Queer? Yes, Lizzie is queer. But as for her being guilty, I say no, and decidedly no."

Emma remembered that on the day of the murders, when she returned from Fairhaven, Lizzie was deeply affected. When the accusations started, she told Emma that "you know that I would not dream of such an awful thing, Emma." Lizzie constantly declared her innocence to Emma when they lived together at Maplecroft. Further, Emma believed that Lizzie's devotion to animals reflected a kind heart that could never harbor such hatred.

In spite of their estrangement, Emma continued to support her sister and to respond to "gossiping persons who seem to take delight in saying cruel things about her." She refused to discuss the reasons for the estrangement, only that she had moved out on the Reverend Edwin Buck's advice. Her attorneys had drawn up an agreement that would allow Lizzie to pay Emma rent and to live at Maplecroft until her death.

Emma had fulfilled the promise made to her mother on her deathbed to always "watch over baby Lizzie." She told Maguire that when she met her mother in the afterlife, her mother would thank her for fulfilling her promise. At that point, Emma was so overcome that she sobbed convulsively. After several minutes, she regained her composure. She said that she was upset with a Fall River newspaper for annually dredging up the tragedy in a "most uncalled review of the case." Every Memorial Day, Emma personally decorated Andrew's and Abby's graves with flowers. Lizzie, on the other hand, sent a florist to do the honors.

At this point, Emma graciously ended the interview. As she ushered the reporter to the door, she said that while the world unfairly persecuted Lizzie, Emma was still her sister's "little mother" and "though we must live as strangers, I will defend Baby Lizzie against merciless tongues."

$$T \quad T \quad T$$

Over the years, the various actors in this tragedy either disappeared into welcome obscurity or gained national prominence. Not much is known about what happened to Lizzie's uncle, John Morse, after the trial. He returned to Iowa and continued farming. He never married and died in Hastings, Iowa, in 1912 at the age of seventy-nine. Over the years, he never spoke about the tragedy. The alleged affair with Lizzie was the imaginative product of an unscrupulous journalist.

Immediately after the trial, Bridget "Maggie" Sullivan moved to New Bedford to work for Joshua Hunt, the New Bedford jailer. A false rumor circulated that Lizzie had paid for Maggie to return to Ireland. In 1905 Maggie moved to Anaconda, Montana, where she married a smelter, John M. Sullivan, and retired to a quiet life as a domestic and wife. Around 1942, she moved to Butte, where she died in 1948 at the approximate age of eighty. She was buried with her husband in Mt. Olivet Cemetery in Anaconda. She never talked about the case.

Edwin McHenry, the notorious private operative, was in and out of trouble with the law and with his wife. After the *Boston Globe* fiasco, he closed up shop in Providence and moved to New York. In 1893, he was arrested for swindling a jeweler out of some expensive items. His wife, Nellie, eventually divorced him for adultery.

Joe Howard, the illustrious New York columnist, returned to New York, where he continued to contribute a column called "Howard's Letter" to the *Boston Globe*. He died on April 1, 1908, in his apartment at the Nevada Hotel in New York. In its obituary, the *Boston Globe* described him as an "aggressive, big-hearted, Bohemian and True-Blue Friend." New York celebrated his life and career with a lavish funeral.

The prosecutor, William Henry Moody, was elected to Congress in 1897. President Theodore Roosevelt appointed him to his cabinet as Secretary of the Navy and then as the United States Attorney General in 1904. In 1906 Roosevelt nominated him to the Supreme Court; he was confirmed later that year. Moody retired in 1909 because of ill health and died in Haverhill, Massachusetts, in 1917. After his death, the navy renamed *Destroyer 277* in his honor.

District Attorney Hosea Knowlton succeeded Arthur Pillsbury as attorney general of Massachusetts in 1894. After he retired, he served on several boards, including those of the Edison Electric Light Company and Citizens National Bank in New Bedford. He died of apoplexy (stroke) in Marion, Massachusetts, in 1902.

Governor George Robinson received $25,000 for defending Lizzie. He returned to his private practice in Chicopee, Massachusetts, and died in 1896. Andrew Jennings became district attorney of Bristol County. To show their gratitude, Emma and Lizzie appointed him to the board of the Globe Yarn Mill that they inherited from their father. He died in 1923.

Lizzie's world grew smaller as her friends died and her sister moved to New Hampshire. She grew obese and more reclusive, preferring her animals to humans. She died on June 1, 1927, in Fall River, at the age of sixty-eight. In the *Boston Globe*, her obituary shared the front page with the Lindbergh flight and the Sacco-Vanzetti case. In the thirty-four years since her trial, the world had radically changed. America had fought a world war, automobiles had replaced the horse and buggy, and women had been granted the right to vote. Lindbergh had flown across the Atlantic, talkies revolutionized motion pictures, and the country would soon experience the Great Depression.

On June 10, 1927, just nine days after Lizzie's death, Emma died in Newmarket, New Hampshire, at the age of seventy-six, reportedly from senility. Both women were buried near their parents in the Oak Grove Cemetery within a week of each other. Not much is known about Lizzie's burial except that an Episcopalian minister read the final words as her body was interred in the Borden lot. According to one possibly apocryphal story, the undertaker called Vida Pearson Turner, a contralto with the Congregational church choir, to report to Maplecroft the morning of the funeral. When she arrived, the undertaker led her into the parlor of the empty house. Alone with Lizzie's possessions, she sang Lizzie's favorite hymn, "In My Ain Countrie," whose words reflected Lizzie's sense of betrayal:

> *The green leaf of loyalty's beginning to fall.*
> *The bonnie White Rose it is withering an' all.*
> *But I'll water it with the blood of usurping tyranny.*
> *And green it will grow in my ain countrie.*

After she finished, the undertaker paid her and swore her to secrecy. Mrs. Turner learned only later that Lizzie had been buried during the night.

Emma's funeral on June 13, 1927, was more publicized. Reverend J. Wynne Jones of Christ Church, Swansea, conducted the service, which was limited to a few family members and friends. Emma, who had left specific directions with her cousin's wife, Mrs. Henry Gardner, several years earlier, had especially requested black pall bearers, an old social custom among prominent families.

The sisters' wills reveal much about Emma's and Lizzie's values and their attitudes toward people and institutions. Lizzie seemed to prize individual loyalty, leaving only a little to institutions except for animal charities. She left a cousin some diamond and amethyst jewelry, her choice of rugs, furniture, and books, and a place in the Oak Grove burial plot. She left her housekeeper the furnishings in her room, and she bequeathed two thousand dollars each to her chauffeur's wife and daughter. Her bequest to Helen Leighton, the founder of the Fall River Animal Rescue League, included diamond and sapphire jewelry, furniture, rugs, books, china, and one-half of her share in the A. J. Borden building in Fall River. She left the Fall River Animal Rescue League $30,000. She left nothing to Emma, claiming that her sister already had a considerable share of her father's estate and was financially solvent. Lizzie also left $5,000 to the City of Fall River for the perpetual care of her father's grave.

Emma was generous with numerous institutions. She left $4,000 to the Fall River Branch of the Association of Collegiate Alumnae, $10,000 to the Home of the Aged, $6,000 to the Salvation Army, and money to several other organizations, including the Boys and Girls Scouts. She also left sizable bequests, including money and personal items, to several relatives. She also acknowledged Andrew J. Jennings's family. If he had survived her, he would have received $1,000 for his dedicated service to the Borden family.

Two images of Lizzie have prevailed over the years: the stoic, cold-hearted murderess, and the generous, kind-hearted woman who funded college education for the less fortunate and championed animal causes. No one has successfully reconciled these seemingly contradictory images. Lizzie was an outsider who never found the acceptance she so desperately desired. Self-righteous churchwomen shunned her after the trial; the reinvented Lizbeth Borden did not behave in a manner that suited them. Her face indicated "the possession of a sort of masculine strength that one does not like to observe in the face of a woman." Was it the murders themselves that particularly disturbed people, or was it her nonconformity?

The Borden mystery continues to baffle and fascinate us. Did Lizzie murder her parents? No one will ever really know. Who might have hated Abby and Andrew Borden enough to murder them in a bloody orgy? Again, we'll never know.

# Lizzie in Popular Culture

O ver the years, the Borden murders have become a significant part of the popular ethos. The case has spawned numerous jingles, books, plays, and of course much speculation. Two books appeared in 1893, shortly after the verdict: *The Mystery Unveiled: The Truth about the Borden Tragedy: Fresh Light That Must Be Convincing to All Readers* by Todd Lunday and *The Fall River Tragedy: History of the Borden Murders* by Edwin Porter, a reporter for the *Fall River Daily Globe*. In his book, Lunday suggested that since no one was convicted of the crime, then no crime occurred. The *Fall River Daily Globe* ridiculed this theory, concluding that "it was simply a case of a fatal combination of excessive heat and cold mutton." Porter's book, not surprisingly, reflected the *Daily Globe's* bias against Lizzie. According to unsubstantiated rumor, Lizzie was so outraged that she purchased and destroyed almost the whole print run.

In spite of the acquittal, popular culture for the most part portrayed Lizzie as a crazed killer. Around the turn of the twentieth century, children started reciting an anonymous jingle that was popular even with President Teddy Roosevelt:

*Lizzie Borden took an ax*
*And gave her mother forty whacks.*
*When she saw what she had done,*
*She gave her father forty-one.*

A. I. Bixby printed a broadside shortly after the trial. It was somewhat more charitable:

*But because your nerve is stout*
*Does not prove beyond a doubt*
*That you knocked the old folks out*
*Lizzie Borden*

Bixby suggested that the public had unfairly condemned Lizzie because of her personality.

Lizzie's tragedy was often dramatized on stage, but often not successfully. In 1934 John Colton and Carlton Miles debuted their play, *Nine Pine Street*, on Broadway with the celebrated actress Lillian Gish as Lizzie. Even Miss Gish couldn't save it. It opened to scathing reviews and closed after a brief run.

Edmund Pearson, one of the earliest Borden experts, published *The Trial of Lizzie Borden* in 1937. Although it contains some excerpts from the trial transcript, some scholars have criticized it for its bias against Lizzie. Pearson published several articles on the Borden case and was involved in a scholarly squabble with Edward Radin over Lizzie's guilt. Radin argued that Maggie murdered the Bordens. In 1948 dancer-choreographer Agnes de Mille staged *Fall River Legend: A Ballet* at the New York Metropolitan Opera House. Critics praised it for capturing the darkness and oppression of the late Victorian era. The "Accused" is portrayed as a sensitive young woman who is driven to murder by a cruel stepmother. A review in *Theatre Arts Magazine* said that the ballet was "a tense emotional experience—so intense as to approach very closely the catharsis attained by any fine work of art." Morton Gould's score sustains the bleak mood, and the ballet's minimalist sets emphasized the bleakness of Victorian life in New England and of Lizzie's plight. The American Ballet Theatre in New York revived the ballet in 1990.

Jack Beeson's opera *Lizzie Borden* opened at the New York City Opera on March 25, 1965. Beeson collaborated with the scenarist Richard Plant and librettist Kenward Elmslie, who created what some critics thought was a complex psychological work. As with most dramatizations of the case, Lizzie is portrayed as a mad assailant. Beeson wrote that "the music, words, and dramatic shape should work together to convince us that Lizzie must murder her parents. If there is any substantial miscalculation, the audience won't go up the stairs with Lizzie—And if they won't go up the stairs, there won't be any point at all in their having come to the theatre." The opera introduces two fictional characters, Jason MacFarlane, a sea captain, and Margret, Lizzie's younger sister, as well as a fictional romantic triangle that engenders a number of violent arguments between Lizzie and her parents. The escalating battles with her parents humiliate Lizzie and drive her further into madness—and ultimately to murder.

On a lighter note, Michael Brown composed "You Can't Chop Your Poppa Up in Massachusetts" for Leonard Sillman's 1952 Broadway revue *New Faces*. Several of the verses are:

*You can't chop your poppa up in Massachusetts*
*Not even if it's planned as a surprise*
*No you can't chop your poppa up in Massachusetts*
*You know how neighbors love to criticize.*

*You can't chop your momma up in Massachusetts,*
*Not even if you're tired of her cuisine.*
*No, you can't chop your mother up in Massachusetts,*
*If you do, you know there's bound to be a scene.*

Reginald Lawrence's *The Legend of Lizzie: A Play in Two Acts* closed on Broadway after two performances in 1959. In 1961 the Chad Mitchell Trio recorded a reinterpreted "hoedown" version of the ditty, which included the words:

*Shut the door and lock and latch it*
*Here comes Lizzie with a brand-new hatchet!*
*Such a snob I heard it said,*

*She met her pa and cut him dead!*
*Jump like a fish—jump like a porpoise,*
*All join hands and habeas corpus!*

Countless authors have offered at times unusual interpretations. Victoria Lincoln in *A Private Disgrace: Lizzie Borden by Daylight* (1967) theorized that Lizzie committed the murder while suffering an epileptic fit. There is no evidence that Lizzie ever suffered from epilepsy or that anyone in an epileptic fit could successfully wield an ax.

The story also made it to television. In 1975 Paul Wendkos directed Elizabeth Montgomery as Lizzie in the television movie *The Legend of Lizzie Borden*. It capitalized on the contemporary rumor that Lizzie stripped naked before committing the murder. The film depicts Lizzie as a dull-witted zombie who went from room to room dragging a bloody ax that she somehow managed to flush down a toilet.

The O. J. Simpson trial in 1996 sparked renewed interest in the murders. The artist Rick Geary published the graphic novel *The Borden Tragedy*, in which many of his overhead frames present a bird's-eye view of the premises. He depicts the murderer in shadow entering the sitting room from the dining room, his or her arm raised with the ax to strike the sleeping Borden. He compared the tragedy to the Simpson case, citing the similar murder weapon, the lack of credible witnesses, the media attention, the short deliberation, and the suspect's wealth.

In addition to the ballets and plays, numerous novelists have offered creative solutions. Marie Belloc Lowndes, in her 1939 novel *Lizzie Borden: A Study in Conjecture*, suggested that Lizzie committed the murders because her stepmother had discovered that she was having an illicit affair with a European lover. In Walter Satterthwait's *Miss Lizzie*, published in 1989, Lizzie solves the murder of her young neighbor's stepmother after World War I. The situation is reversed, reinventing Lizzie as the detective heroine who solves the crime.

The house on Second Street has since become a popular and successful bed-and-breakfast. Borden enthusiasts tour the house, spend the night in Morse's or Lizzie's room, and awaken to a breakfast similar to what Mrs. Borden served. Borden memorabilia is on sale in a gift shop:

bobble-head dolls, hatchet earrings, and cat figurines commemorating Lizzie's devotion to animals. While curious tourists risk the rumored meandering of ghosts, popular culture continues to reinvent Lizzie, and scholars work to solve the unsolved.

# BIBLIOGRAPHY

Brown, Arnold R. *Lizzie Borden: The Legend, the Truth, the Final Chapter.* Nashville: Rutledge Hill Press, 1991.

Commonwealth of Massachusetts v. Lizzie A. Borden; *The Knowlton Papers, 1892-1893.* Eds. Michael Martins and Dennis A. Binette. Fall River, Mass.: Fall River Historical Society, 1994.

Davis, Judge Charles G. "The Conduct of the Law in the Borden Case." *Boston Daily Advertiser,* 1894.

de Mille, Agnes. *Lizzie Borden: A Dance of Death.* Boston: Little, Brown, 1968.

Geary, Rick. *The Borden Tragedy: A Memoir of the Infamous Double Murder at Fall River, Massachusetts, 1892.* New York: NBN, 1997.

Kent, David. *Forty Whacks: New Evidence in the Life and Legend of Lizzie Borden.* Emmaus: Yankee Books, 1992.

_____. *Lizzie Borden Sourcebook.* Boston: Brandon, 1992.

Lincoln, Victoria. *A Private Disgrace: Lizzie Borden by Daylight.* New York: G. P. Putnam's Sons, 1967.

*Lizzie Borden: Did She? . . . Or . . . Didn't She?* Verplanck: Historical Briefs, 1992.

Lunday, Todd. *The Mystery Unveiled: The Truth about the Borden Tragedy: Fresh Light That Must Be Convincing to All Readers.* Providence: J. A. & R. A. Reid, 1893.

Masterson, William L. *Lizzie Didn't Do It!* Boston: Brandon, 2000.

Pearson, Edmund. *The Trial of Lizzie Borden.* New York: Doubleday, 1937.

Porter, Edwin H. *The Fall River Tragedy: History of the Borden Murders.* Fall River, Mass.: Press of J. D. Munroe, 1893.

Radin, Edward. *Lizzie Borden: The Untold Story*. New York: Simon & Schuster, 1961.

Rebello, Leonard. *Lizzie Borden: Past and Present*. Ai-Zach Press, 1999.

Samuels, Charles, and Louise Samuels. *The Girl in the House of Hate: The Story and All the Facts of the Lizzie Borden Murders*. New York: Fawcett, 1953.

Spiering, Frank. *Lizzie: The Story of Lizzie Borden*. New York: Random House, 1984.

Sullivan, Robert. *Goodbye Lizzie Borden*. Brattleboro, Vt.: Stephen Greene Press, 1974.

# INDEX